About this Book

This book shows you how to be your own boss. It tells you how to start your own business. It covers all the basics to get you going on your own road to independence.

Learn where to get ideas for a business. How to do your own research and where to get information. How to plan your business.

Why location is so important. Learn about human resources and the basic concepts in marketing and advertising. Find out how to price your product or service and how to prepare financial projections.

Can you afford to finance the business start-up or will the business be able to finance itself once it is up and running? Find out where to obtain outside capital. Learn what's involved in borrowing.

Why cash management and cost control are so important. Finally, take a look at ways to expand your business and reach that pot of gold at the end of the rainbow.

About the Author

Iain Williamson is an entrepreneur, business consultant and seminar leader. His views have appeared in many newspaper articles. He has also been a guest on radio and has appeared on television shows such as: CBC TV's *Venture*; TVO's *MoneysWorth*, and *Canada Tonight* of BCTV and CHCH Television.

Iain spent five years as a financial analyst and knows what makes business tick. For over 20 years he operated his own businesses in importing, high technology and manufacturing. He is now a small business consultant and also owns a book publishing business. He writes from his personal experience in the trenches, as an entrepreneur and consultant, and shares these insights with you.

Iain holds degrees from the Universities of St. Andrew's in Scotland and Oxford in England.

If you want to be your own boss and run your own business, this book should be at the top of your **must read** list.

Start Your Own Business - Be Your Own Boss!

Your Road Map to Independence

THE BOSS

Iain Williamson

ISBN: 1-896210-96-1

This book is dedicated to Vicki for all her help.

Written by:
Iain Williamson,
Entrepreneurial Business Consultants of Canada,
P.O. Box 7200, Station A, Toronto, Ont. M5W 1X8
Phone: (416) 322-9896

Published in Canada by:
Productive Publications, P.O. Box 7200,
Station A, Toronto, Ont. M5W 1X8
Phone: (416) 483-0634   Fax: (416) 322-7434

Copyright © 1999 by Iain Williamson

National Library of Canada cataloguing

Williamson, Iain

     Start your own business, be your own boss! : your
roadmap to independence

ISBN 1-896210-96-1

     1. New business enterprises.   I. Title

HD62.5.W48 1999   658.1'1   C98-900841-X

GET YOUR FREE CATALOGUE OF BOOKS TO HELP <u>YOU</u> SUCCEED

✔ YES, <u>rush</u> me your FREE Catalogue. I am interested in:
- ☐ How to Start My Own Business
- ☐ Find Growth Capital
- ☐ Export Successfully
- ☐ Make Money Selling by Direct Mail
- ☐ Protect My Inventions
- ☐ How to Cut My Taxes
- ☐ How I Can Get a Better Job
- ☐ How Can I Profit from the Internet

Fill in your name and address on the reverse side and mail now ⇒

FOR YOUR COPY OF THE LATEST FREE CATALOGUE:
Mail Card Now or Call 1-800-829-1317 in Canada (24 hrs.)
Or From the U.S. Call 1-800-850-4636 (24 hrs.)

GET YOUR FREE CATALOGUE OF BOOKS TO HELP <u>YOU</u> SUCCEED

✔ YES, <u>rush</u> me your FREE Catalogue. I am interested in:
- ☐ How to Start My Own Business
- ☐ Find Growth Capital
- ☐ Export Successfully
- ☐ Make Money Selling by Direct Mail
- ☐ Protect My Inventions
- ☐ How to Cut My Taxes
- ☐ How I Can Get a Better Job
- ☐ How Can I Profit from the Internet

Fill in your name and address on the reverse side and mail now ⇒

Name:_____

Title:_____

Organization:_____

Address:_____

City:_____

Province/State & Code:_____

Phone:_____

PRODUCTIVE PUBLICATIONS
P.O. Box 7200, Station A
Toronto, ON
M5W 1X8
Canada

FOR YOUR COPY OF THE LATEST FREE CATALOGUE:
Mail Card Now or Call 1-800-829-1317 in Canada (24 hrs.)
Or From the U.S. Call 1-800-850-4636 (24 hrs.)

Name:_____

Title:_____

Organization:_____

Address:_____

City:_____

Province/State & Code:_____

Phone:_____

PRODUCTIVE PUBLICATIONS
P.O. Box 7200, Station A
Toronto, ON
M5W 1X8
Canada

For Your Copy of the Latest Free Catalogue: Mail Card Now or Call 1-800-829-1317 (24 hrs.)

From the U.S. Call 1-800-850-4636 (24 Hrs.)

CONTENTS

CHAPTER 1

INTRODUCTION

CHAPTER 2

BE YOUR OWN BOSS!

CHAPTER 3

WHERE TO GET GREAT IDEAS

CHAPTER 4

HOW TO RESEARCH YOUR IDEAS

CHAPTER 5

PLANNING YOUR BUSINESS

CHAPTER 6

LOCATION, LOCATION, LOCATION

CHAPTER 7

HUMAN RESOURCES

Contents

CHAPTER 8

MARKETING AND ADVERTISING

CHAPTER 9

PRICING YOUR PRODUCT OR SERVICE

CHAPTER 10

FINANCIAL PROJECTIONS

CHAPTER 11

DO YOU HAVE ENOUGH MONEY?

Contents

CHAPTER 12

SEEKING OUTSIDE INVESTORS

CHAPTER 13

BORROWING MONEY FOR YOUR BUSINESS

CHAPTER 14

CASH MANAGEMENT

CHAPTER 15

COST CONTROL

CHAPTER 16

EXPANDING

CHAPTER 17

THE POT OF GOLD

CHAPTER 18

CONCLUSION

1

INTRODUCTION

Congratulations!

You've taken the first step to being your own boss!

This will be a long and exciting journey for you and I hope that I can help you based on my many years of experience in running my own businesses. I started back in May, 1974, after leaving a job as a financial analyst in the stockbrokerage business.

I must confess, that when I first started, I felt that I knew everything about how to run a business, since I had been analyzing how other people ran their businesses for the previous five years. I had also been telling institutional investors how those businesses run and why some would be successful and some would fail.

It was the some shock that I found out that I did not know everything, since running your own business requires a multitude of different skills. You have to be your own a marketing manager, bookkeeper, financial analyst, production manager, human resource manager, typist, brochure designer, manager of accounts receivable and accounts payable, the public relations manager, customer service manager, manager in charge of cleaning floors, new product development, manager of... everything!

Meanwhile you have got to keep up with developments in technology... keep an eye on your competitors... pay your taxes... fill out all those government forms... and make sure that you are making money.

You have to be prepared, when you start your own business, to be Jack of all Trades. Unfortunately, most of us do not have the time to acquire the skills when we're working for somebody else and find ourselves in a situation of trying to bring ourselves up to par at a very stressful time in our lives. Indeed, starting a new business can be an exhilarating experience, but it can also place huge demands on our everyday life and those associated with us.

What I started out on my own, I had little concept of what lay ahead, however, I did learn through hard experience what to do right and what to avoid. This was a painful learning experience and I had a couple of businesses go under beneath me (although they did not go bankrupt). But, I gained courage from the fact that a gentleman by the name of Macy had gone into bankruptcy four times before starting a department store in New York in which he had insisted that his customers would receive no credit and would pay on the barrel. The rest was history.

They say that experience is knowing that you made that mistake once before. There is much truth in that statement, however, you'll never learn anything new without making mistakes. Show me the skier that slalomed down the hill with great elegance the first time they donned a pair of skis. Most of us skiers learned how to ski by falling repeatedly. As a novice, I even remember going down the slope backwards and the only way I could stop myself was by falling over!

Very few people get it right the first time and even those people who claim success will probably hide the fact that they made many mistakes on the way.

From my own viewpoint, I wish that I had been able to get my hands on a book that told me what to do and how to do it. Now that I have had some success in running my own businesses, I can clearly see what I did wrong, when I first started.

Hopefully, this book will help to reduce the number of those early mistakes and help you to jump start your new enterprise. It should help to put you on the right course even though a short book such as this, cannot tell you everything and I would encourage you to read as much as you can before you embark on your new enterprise and to do your research as thoroughly as you can.

Running your own business can be a very exciting experience... but seeing it fall from for the sky can be a devastating experience. Sometimes there is a very fine line between success and failure and when you, as a new entrepreneur, has to attend to so many things at once, it is possible to overlook that one alligator that will nip you in the behind.

Like the soldier going to war, you have to be alert on all fronts and be prepared for the unexpected. You will find that very few things go exactly according to plan and you will have to be very versatile in the way in which you plan your strategy and carry through.

This book will cover most of factors that you should consider when you go into business for the first time. However, it must be remembered that every business is different and requires a different approach. It is a challenge in a book such as this to cover all eventualities for every type of enterprise. Once again I would encourage you to read as much as you can about the type of business you intend to stat before you jump into it.

This book will be most useful to you when you read it carefully and reflect upon the points raised and how they will apply to the particular type of business that you intend to start. This way you'll get the maximum benefit out of what the following chapters have to offer.

2

BE YOUR OWN BOSS!

The Ugly Side of the New Global Economy

All of us are being affected in one way or another by the "New Global Economy". It brings with it many advantages such as cheaper goods from overseas markets where labour costs are much lower than in Canada and the United States. It also brings with it all the technological "goodies" that come out of research laboratories such as better drugs, lower telecommunications costs, high-definition television, DVD's, and so on.

In spite of this, there is a very ugly side to the New Global Economy. Thus, many multinational companies are moving their labour-intensive operations to low wage paying countries in an effort to cut costs. The result of this is that many loyal employees with many years of devoted service to their companies, are being put out on the trash heap.

A classic example of this is the garment industry, which has been moving offshore over the last decade. This trend continues as was illustrated recently with the announcement by Levi, the jeans manufacturer, that they would be closing many of their American plants and opening up in low wage cost areas overseas.

Competitive pricing pressures of the New Global Economy are forcing companies to slash their domestic labour costs in order to become more efficient. They are replacing people with automated machinery, robots and computers that can perform the same tasks at much less cost (even allowing for maintenance and the need for highly skilled operators).

This trend has been going on for many years. Thus, I remember going to a trade show in Chicago about 15 years ago and listing to a seminar where a company that painted golf balls was discussing their new robotic painting system. Whilst I cannot remember the exact figures, to the President of the company showed us how he could triple his production with a single robot. Not only that, his wastage was greatly reduced. With the previous manual system, a large number of golf balls were inadvertently dropped on the floor and had to be recycled into the system. The robots did not drop any balls, thereby eliminating all of the recycling.

It is Only Going to Get Uglier

Unfortunately, the end is not in sight for the elimination of jobs by companies seeking to become leaner and meaner in the New Economy. Thus, the Internet and the new information highway is causing many companies to rethink the way in which they do business.

A classic example of this is Dell computers. Approximately half of their current sales are being made directly over the Internet to the end user. This is in contrast to the traditional computer manufacturer which sends its products to a distributor; which in turn sells them to a retailer; who in turn sells them to the end user.

This is a very interesting case, because the manufacturer or assembler of the computer is selling direct to the end user, thereby eliminating both the distributor and the retailer. This process is known as "disintermediation", in which the middleman is eliminated.

Another example is Egghead Computers in the United States which formerly operated about 90 retail stores which sold software. In an effort to become more profitable, the company decided to close its retail stores and sell its products directly over the Internet. I understand that this has resulted in a reduction of total revenue, however, it appears to have increased the company's profitability.

In the Egghead case, the software belongs to other software companies and Egghead is not involved in its preparation, but in its sale to the end user. In this instance, Egghead is using the Internet as a retail sales mechanism that eliminates the need for brick and mortar stores, together with all the associated costs.

Think about this for a minute! No longer does Egghead have to pay substantial rents for high visibility retail outlets. No longer does it have to pay all of the costs associated with retailing such as utilities, in-store security, in-store signage, municipal taxes, store displays.... in fact, Egghead can now operate out of a low-cost location, with far fewer employees.

Both of the above examples involving Dell and Egghead illustrate accelerating tends in our new information age economy. You will note the high degree of efficiency with which these companies are able to serve their customers directly without large amounts of real estate and with far fewer people involved in the selling process. Thus, Dell has bypassed all the people that would be required in a distribution and retail network; whereas Egghead has directly reduced its staff and improved its profitability.

These trends towards greater efficiency, also have a darker side.

What is happening is that companies are further reducing the number of people that are employed (either directly or indirectly) in selling their products to the end user. The end result will be more and more lost jobs.

You may very well ask why unemployment rates in both the United States and Canada have declined to their lowest levels in many years. However, you should examine where most of the new jobs are being created. A large portion of them are in low paying, service industry jobs. If you look at the trends over the last 20 years you will see a dramatic shift away from manufacturing towards low paying "hamburger-flipping" jobs.

To be fair, I have to admit that there is a great scarcity of people with the skills required in the area of computers, programming and electronics. Indeed, colleges and universities cannot produce these people fast enough to meet the market demand. On the other hand, there are millions upon millions of workers who do not have (and probably will never be able to acquire) the necessary skills to fill these jobs.

With the exception of high tech jobs, most workers face a very uncertain future even if they are lucky enough to have a job at the moment. Those in manufacturing with high-paying jobs with uncertain futures could find themselves either out of work or facing the prospect of flipping hamburgers in a grease pit for the rest of their lives!

It should also be remembered that not all new jobs created by technology are wonderful, high-paying jobs. This was clearly illustrated a number of years ago in Toronto, where a well known pizza chain had its workers go on strike in protest because the company was employing home workers to answer their phones and process the orders. The coverage in the press suggested that these workers were

8

receiving less than minimum wage, because they were being paid on a per-call basis. In other words, the company had created an "electronic sweat shop".

The Entrepreneurial Alternative

The alternatives for many laid-off workers and those with uncertain futures are fairly straightforward. They can either seek government support, retire early, try to find another job in an increasingly competitive job market, or start their own business.

In addition, wages in recent years have remained relatively stagnant whereas children's college education, new housing, automobiles etc., have been creeping steadily upward, in spite of assurances from politicians and government officials that inflation is under control. This has led many families and individuals to "moonlight" at a second and sometimes even a third job in order to stay ahead. Many such people may be looking to start a business on the side, in order to supplement their meagre wage packet.

Hopefully, this book will help both the full-time and the part-time entrepreneur in setting up their business and in helping them to address some of the critical issues that they will have to face.

What Business Structure is Suitable for You?

Before taking a look at the advantages and disadvantages of being your own boss, it would be helpful to consider what type of business is suitable for your situation. In this context, we are considering the legal structure of the business, rather than the activities it is engaged in. There are tax implications and you should seek professional advice.

The first type of business is a sole proprietorship. Here, you simply register the name of your business with the government for a relatively modest fee. You are then free to use the name which you have chosen and conduct business under that name.

The second type of business is a partnership which can involve two or more people. Under this type of arrangement the partners sign a partnership agreement which defines their ownership and responsibilities. Again, this type of business is relatively easy to form and aside from the legal costs associated with the partnership agreement, registration fees are normally very modest.

The third type of business arrangement is to incorporate. This creates a separate legal entity which can have its own bank accounts and conduct business and enter into contracts as if it were an individual. The incorporated company is owned by the shareholders, who are issued shares reflecting their ownership. In addition, the incorporated company is expected to appoint a board of directors. The board responsible for determining the overall policies and directions of the company in addition to appointing the officers who run the company, such as the president, secretary, vice-president of finance, etc. The board is also responsible for appointing outside advisers such as, accountants, attorneys or lawyers.

In a number of jurisdictions, it is possible for only one person to be the shareholder. In such case that person would appoint themselves as the single member of the board and occupy the positions of president and secretary.

In the United States it is also possible to establish what is known as a "C-Corporation", which allows the entrepreneur to start off in a proprietorship mode and then to switch to a corporate status once the company has advanced beyond the start-up stage.

The Advantages of Being Your Own Boss

There are many advantages in running your own business. Let us take a look at a few of them.

The first is that you are accountable only to yourself, however, this only applies if you are a sole proprietor or run a limited company without other shareholders or a board of directors.

The second relates to your level off stress. I remember a number of years ago hearing about a study conducted on a number of big corporations in which they found the presidents of the companies had far fewer heart attacks than the vice presidents or other managers. The president, being in charge, can "download" his workload to subordinates and it is these subordinates that are in the pressure cooker for getting things completed.

As owner of your own business, you will find that there are many tax advantages. This is especially the case with home-based entrepreneurs, who can write-off a portion of their rent or mortgage payment as a business expense. The portion that can be written off is calculated according to the amount of space that is used in actively conducting the business compared to the total space of the dwelling..

Owners can also write-off a portion off their entertainment expenses, provided that these are directly related to furthering the business. The portion that is allowed will vary from jurisdiction to jurisdiction.

Business owners can also claim their automobile expenses relating to the distances driven while conducting company business. You can usually write-off a portion of your leasing costs if the vehicle is leased, or you can write-off or amortize a portion of the capital costs according to the tax laws prevailing in your state, province, or territory.

Many jurisdictions also allow small businesses a much more favourable tax rate than their larger counterparts. In this regard, it will behove you to seek professional advice from a tax accountant.

Probably the greatest advantage to running your own business is the sense of self-satisfaction that can be obtained from running your own show. I can certainly relate to this myself, when after five years as a financial analyst in the stockbrokerage business. While there, I found that hardly anybody would praise you when you made a good call, but they heaped on piles of scorn anytime you made the slightest error. I think I had a pretty good record and I worked very hard and in the end it wasn't the pay, but it was the people that made me quit the brokerage business for good.

If you work for somebody else who doesn't appreciate what you're doing, I'm sure that you will feel the same way as I did. There will probably be many times when you ask yourself "why am I working for these jerks?". This is the time when entrepreneurship makes a lot of sense as a career alternative.

Once you get your business onto a stable footing and you find yourself madly trying to keep up with a rush of orders, you will start to feel a sense of deep internal satisfaction that you have created something worthwhile. Hopefully, the advice contained in this book will help you reach that stage.

The Disadvantages of Being Your Own Boss

On the flip-side of the coin, there are quite a few disadvantages attached to being your own boss.

The first and most obvious is the absence of a regular paycheck. What you do in your own business and how successful you are at it will determine what you make financially. If your business is not profitable, or if you have to plow all the profits back into the business in order to sustain its growth, you may not be able to pay yourself any salary. This should caution the new entrepreneur that many months, or even years may go by until the business is generating enough money to draw a decent salary. This in turn, means that you have to have enough resources to sustain yourself during the initial start-up phase.

The second relates to those who work for you. In the first place it is often difficult to find employees who will be loyal to you during the start-up initial phase of your business. In my experience, most employees are just interested in the cheque on payday and unless they have some interest (in the form of ownership or some kind of participation in the company's profits), their loyalty is as fickle as the next job offer from some other company. Indeed, finding good employees is one of the most critical challenges facing the new business owner.

The new business owner also has a responsibility toward his employees. Thus, he has to make sure that there is enough money in the bank to cover every payroll. This can make many a new business owner sweat blood when they find that there is hardly enough money to pay their employees. Believe me, they will walk out the door the instant they get wind of the fact that the business is in financial trouble. So, as somebody once remarked to me many years ago, the initiation for any new business owner is being able to meet the company payroll on a regular basis.

As boss, you're also responsible for the safety and proper working conditions for your employees. If these are not met, you will find government or municipal officials swarming down on you like a killer bees. This reminds me of someone I know who runs his own business and who operated a forklift that was powered by natural gas. For some reason the fuel was not burning properly and was emitting poisonous fumes. This resulted in the plant being shut down and all the employees rushed in an ambulance bus to the nearest hospital for examination. Subsequently, the inspectors gave the owner a very hard time for not providing a safe work environment for his employees, even though the accident was caused through no-fault of his own.

As owner, you have to be prepared to accept responsibility, not only for the work environment, but also for the products or services which you produce or offer. You are also responsible for the actions of employees. Thus, if an angry employee punches a customer in the nose because they were complaining about something, you, as owner of the business, could also be held legally responsible for the action of that employee.

The same thing would apply if a customer comes to visit your business location, and trips on a loose paving stone leading to your front door (assuming it is on your business property) you could be sued for the medical expenses incurred by that customer, together with any damages that the courts may award. In the event that the customer badly smashed up his knee and suffered a disability for life, such damages could be very substantial.

I remember a case in a business that I ran a number of years ago in which we had installed a security surveillance camera in a jewellery store which took a picture every time somebody entered the store. It was the responsibility of the store owner or manager to replace the film in the camera at certain regular intervals when the roll film had been used up. It was therefore with some surprise that I found myself, as owner of the business, being sued for some high-priced figurines which were stolen by a shoplifter, on the basis that the camera had malfunctioned at the time of the theft! Eventually, it turned out that the store manager had not replaced the film since the camera had been installed! We were able to prove this in court and the case was dismissed.

I relate these stories to show you that, as boss, you have a lot of responsibilities. In the case of the jewellery store theft, I carried liability insurance for my products and the insurance company provided me with a lawyer to fight the case on my behalf. However, it still took quite a lot of my time to defend the action, since it was in an out-of-town location. The moral of this story is to carry adequate liability insurance for your business and to make sure that your personal financial affairs are arranged in such a way as to protect your financial assets in the event that a successful court action is levied against you. Such arrangements could include the transfer of major assets into the name of a spouse or to consider placing funds in a foreign location, such as a tax haven, which could also act to protect you in the event of unforseen litigation.

With regard to financing your business growth, you will find that most lenders (banks in particular) are very reluctant to lend money to a proprietorship. They by far prefer to deal with incorporated companies. This is also true for investments from informal investors as well as venture capitalists.

The same disadvantage applies to partnerships, however, in this case there is a double jeopardy because each partner is responsible for the financial actions of the other. Thus, if one partner causes the company to lose a great deal of money and is unable to cover that loss, the other partner or partners will be legally responsible to make up for the loss, even though they were not immediately responsible for it. So, you should be aware of potential problems such as this before you enter into a partnership agreement with any other person or persons.

Also, in the case of a partnership, you are only a "co-boss" to the extent of your ownership in the partnership. Indeed, this can lead to a great deal of friction between the partners and many partnerships do not survive the test of time.

In theory, the incorporated company has limited liability for its actions. Thus, it could run into financial difficulty and get into a situation where it cannot pay its bills. In a case such as this, the company could go into receivership or declare bankruptcy without affecting the business owner. In practice, however, the business owner is legally responsible for sales and other taxes that are owed to the government. The owner can also be held responsible for unpaid employees wages, however, this depends upon the jurisdiction in which the business is located.

When an incorporated company loans money from a bank (or other lender), the owner usually has to personally guarantee the loan. This means, that if the business fails, the owner can find himself or herself on the hook for the amount of money that is owing by the business. In this regard, I know of a case which came to my attention recently, in which the owner found he was unable to pay his bills and decided to close the business down. Recognizing the problem that he faced with respect to his personal guarantees on the bank's loan to his business, he very shrewdly continued to run the business while he scrambled to collect his accounts receivable (i.e., the money owing his business), in order to pay off the bank. He also eliminated his personal liabilities with respect to taxes owing by the business. I am happy to say that he was successful in these efforts before he finally closed the business down.

What this goes to show is that the limited liability protection offered by an incorporated company is quite meaningless when it comes to debt obligations to lenders and tax obligations to the government. It can, however, offer protection with respect to amounts owing to unsecured creditors such as, suppliers, landlords, etc.

16

In the case of a limited liability company, the "boss" may be responsible to a board of directors or to the shareholders of the company if a majority of the shares are not held by himself or herself. In practice, however, the president of many such companies carry on regardless of the opinions of the board and of the shareholders. However, it must be remembered that if push comes to shove, a majority of the voting shareholders of a company can replace the president and the board in a company, according to corporate law.

Lastly, on a personal level you will probably find that your new business consumes all of your time, leaving very little for family or social affairs. This can place a considerable strain on the relationships with those around you and it is something that you should consider before you embark on any new entrepreneurial adventure.

In order to succeed, you'll have be prepared to make a lot of sacrifices. Most of these involve the amount of time that will be required to make your business grow. You will find that running your own business is not a 9 a.m. to 5 p.m. affair. It involves very long hours and it is not uncommon for business owners to put in 80 hours or more per week. This is something to think about if you have heavy family obligations or other responsibilities that would prevent you from putting in the hours that you will need to turn your business into something that is profitable.

The above list of disadvantages is by no means complete, however, most of them are not insurmountable, especially if you are aware in advance of their existence and are prepared to meet the challenges head-on.

3

WHERE TO GET GREAT IDEAS

Ideas Abound!

In this chapter we will examine a number of ways in which to get ideas that you can use to create a business. If you have already made up your mind on what you want to do, you may wish to skip this chapter.

Ideas abound around us and the key to finding something that will make a good business that would be a good fit for you is to go through an initial process of self-examination. Most people would like to work at something which they enjoy even though it may involve a great deal of effort. Thus, a person who loves the outdoors and nature might want to take a look at the area of eco-tourism. Equally well, a person who enjoys golf might want to take a look at products or services (such as a golf driving range), which relate to that area.

Another factor to consider in self-examination, is to self-evaluate your own strengths and weaknesses. Thus, if you are a very outgoing person and enjoy other people's company, you probably have most of what it takes to be involved in selling a product or service. On the other hand, if you are very shy and introverted you might want to consider a business in which the selling and promotion can be done through direct mail, the Internet or by employing skilled salespeople to do the selling. Much of this self-examination is very similar to what people go through in career counselling. In fact, it may be a good idea to seek career counselling in order to establish your strengths and weaknesses and then apply these to the type of business that you want to start.

Now, let us consider a number of ways in which to get ideas for your business. The following sections do not cover every possibility, but they will certainly give you a good handle on how to get started. My advice is to select those which offer the best chances of finding something that fits in with your interests and the self-evaluation which you have conducted. You may find several areas which would be of interest and I would suggest that you list these. There is certainly no harm in looking at a variety of different areas and in the following chapters I will try to help you in doing market research into these areas and to establish which ones would be the most profitable for you to enter into.

Trade Shows

In my own experience, I found trade shows to be a tremendous source of inspiration for new ideas or for ways to start a business.

Essentially, trade shows are of two types. These are those that are open to the public, such as many of the sportsman's shows, food shows, automobile shows and boat shows, etc., and these are held (usually on an annual basis) in major centers around the country. They are easy to gain access to... all you have to do is pay the entrance fee and you are admitted.

The other type of trade shows are those which specialize in specific industries or services and are intended only for people that work in these areas. In other words, admission is not open to the general public and for that reason I would strongly suggest that you prepare yourself by registering the name of your company and having business cards printed. Often, a business card is all that is needed to gain admission onsite, however, there is usually an admission fee.

An alternative is to contact the show organizers in advance and request a show registration form which you can complete and mail or fax it back to the organizer who will then mail you your admission badge. In order to contact the show organizers, I would recommend that you visit your local reference library and they should be able to supply you with directories of trade shows that are held both in North America and throughout the world.

In the past, I visited many trade shows in Europe, and I have found these to be a great source of inspiration for new business ideas or for the creation of new products. Also, many of the products that were on display were not available in North America and this offered many opportunities to act as a North American distributor or wholesaler. So, I would strongly recommend some foreign travel, if you can afford it, because the further you get away from home, the more ideas you are likely to find that have not already been developed in your home market.

Many of these trade shows are gigantic in size and I would highly recommend that you plan your visit carefully. Some shows will mail the exhibitor list in advance or alternatively you can obtain it when you register at the show opening. My suggestion is to go through the list of exhibitors and carefully select those whose products or services you would be most interested in. You can then the target those companies. To make this easier, most trade shows include a booth layout plan in their exhibitor catalogue which permits you to plan your visits in an organized fashion.

Another alternative is to spend the first day (or two) quickly visiting the booths without getting involved in any detailed discussions with the salespeople, and make notes on which booths contain products or services that would be of interest to you.

In the evenings, you can go through any literature or sales material that you of obtained from those booths tat were of interest and further narrow down your choices. Having done this, you can visit just those companies that meet your criteria and get into detailed discussions with them. Don't forget to exchange business cards and also be aware that the people manning these booths are trained salespeople who want to close the sale, so be on guard and do not commit yourself to anything until you have had a chance to do your own research and investigate the area more thoroughly. In the next chapter I will show you how to do this.

When you get back home after the show is over, I would recommend that you go through all literature that you collected. Carefully select anything that would be of interest, even if it involves competitors products, because such information could be very valuable to you later on. Organize the material and file it away.

Trade Magazines

Once you have selected the area or areas that you are interested in starting a business, I would strongly recommend that you subscribe to the trade magazines that relate to that area. The publishers of many of these magazines will also have booths at the trade shows that relate to them and if you subscribe at the show you may be able to obtain such magazines at a discounted price or for free if you meet their circulation criteria (i.e., that you are actively involved in that industry or service since your subscription is being subsidized by the paid advertising contained in the magazine).

I would also suggest that you visit your local reference library which will probably have a number of trade magazines on display. Alternatively, they should be able to provide you with directories that will list trade magazines. Many of these directories are designed to provide information about advertising rates, however, they will also provide you with contact addresses, phone and fax numbers so that you can subscribe.

Don't forget to look at foreign publications relating to the area that you're interested in. Thus, there are many trade publications in English that come from Hong Kong, Taiwan, United Kingdom and other English speaking nations that will give you a different perspective on the area that is of interest to you.

Retail Stores

The shops in your neighbourhood can be a great source of inspiration for new products. Visit your local shopping mall and you will find millions of ideas for products that sell. You will also see many successful chains that are leaders in their field. These will give you some idea of what is involved in merchandising and selling products.

I would suggest that take a small notebook with you and make notes on products or stores that are interest to you. Be careful not to do this blatantly in front of sales clerks, but rather do it discreetly after you have exited the store. Also, do not attempt to photograph anything, especially in shopping malls, since you will attract the attention of mall security very quickly. Simply put, retailers welcome you as a shopper but become very hostile if they feel that you are spying on them.

Again, if you have the money to travel, it would be a good idea to examine the merchandise in stores in foreign countries, since these can be a great inspiration for new products that are not available in your local market.

Catalogues

There are literally thousands upon thousands of catalogues available. I would classify these into two broad categories: those put out by catalogue companies that are selling merchandise which you can purchase directly from the catalogue and those that are put out by manufacturers, distributors, or wholesalers which contain information for those further down the distribution system. Thus, a manufacturer of widgets might produce a catalogue which describes the full range of widgets that are produced so that businesses which sell widgets can be made aware of what is available and how to order them.

Again, depending on the type of business that you're interested in, you can obtain copies of these catalogues. The easiest of these to obtain a those put out by the companies selling merchandise, since most of them would gladly send you a copy upon your request in the hope that you will become a customer. The more difficult types of catalogue to obtain are those put out by manufacturers, distributors or wholesalers since, these are restricted to businesses that are either existing customers or are potential customers and you will have to have a pretty good reason in order to obtain a copy.

Advertisements, Brochures and Fliers

Most homes and businesses are inundated with unsolicited advertising in the form of brochures and fliers which extole the virtues of some product or service. The fact that people in your local area are making money offering these products and services, should alert you to many potential opportunities that you might not otherwise have considered.

Also, when you are reading a newspaper or magazine, pay attention to the advertisements. These will display many new products that can be of interest to you.

Hobbies

If you already have a hobby, such as stamp collecting or collecting antiques, you might want to consider developing this further into a business. There are many advantages to doing this, because you will already be familiar with the area and you will have less learning to do in order to get started. You will also be familiar with the current methods of selling and distribution.

Another advantage with developing a hobby into a business for those who are already working somewhere else, is that you can start the business slowly in your spare time until it has developed to such a stage that it can support you on a full-time basis.

Libraries

Your local reference library is a goldmine of business ideas and opportunities. Most reference sections contain directories of manufacturers, service companies and many specialized areas which are full of information that you can use to get business ideas.

Aside from directories, many large libraries have extensive business sections, and you may very well find books written by authorities in your area of interest.

Many big libraries also subscribe to leading trade journals which you can examine. Even if they do not have anything relating to your area of interest, they will probably be able to supply you with a directory of trade journals (as discussed earlier).

Foreign Trade Commissioners

Whilst the embassies of most large foreign countries are located in the capital city such as, Washington in the case of the United States, or Ottawa in the case of Canada, consulates are often located in major cities around the country. Most consulates have trade attachés who are responsible for developing trade opportunities with their home country. Such attachés can be a valuable source of information for companies that are seeking local representation.

In addition, many consulates also maintain a small reference library with directories from the home country. Because of security concerns (associated with bombings and demonstrations), you would be well advised to make an appointment in advance with the librarian.

Telephone Yellow Pages

The sections in your local Yellow Pages are full of business ideas. If you skim through your local book, you will likely come up with many ideas which fit your criteria.

If you have access to a large reference library, you may find that they have Yellow Pages for most major cities and possibly for some overseas cities as well. It may well be worth spending a day going through these directories because you will find all sorts of ideas for starting a business.

The Internet

The Internet is akin to a huge world library with information on millions upon millions of topics. I would very strongly suggest that you take the time to surf the World Wide Web and use the search engines to select the areas that you're interested in.

You will also find that many companies have their own Web sites or Web pages which contain information about the products and services that they offer. Again, these can be great sources for business ideas.

Just Look Around You!

In the above text I have covered some of the more obvious ways in which to get business ideas. I am sure that, if you work it is, you will find many more and my advice to you is to keep your eyes open and look around you! You will find business ideas almost everywhere you look.

Store Your Ideas

Even if you have selected an idea for your business, it is still worthwhile maintaining a filing cabinet (or even a cardboard box) containing the ideas which you have collected. You may be able to incorporate some of these into the business that you start, or in the event that you have selected an idea which does not work out, you can always fall back on the ideas which you previously collected.

4

HOW TO RESEARCH YOUR IDEAS

Get a Feel for the Market

Before you rush out and open a store or a manufacturing facility, you should try to get a "gut feeling" for the market. This can be accomplished by means of a market survey.

The importance of such a survey cannot be overemphasized. It is of paramount importance. It is an essential step in the preparation of a marketing plan, which in turn, becomes an essential element of your business strategy and should be incorporated into your business plan (more about this in a later chapter).

You must find out how your proposed product or service stands in relation to those of your competitors. It is also essential to know whether the total market for the product or service is growing or declining. There is no use opening up a plant that manufactures manual typewriters because soon they will only be found in museums.

Market surveys of new products, especially in the high technology and biotechnology areas, can be extremely difficult to conduct. This arises because of their novel nature and because markets may not yet have been established for them. In other words, these are products looking for a market.

On account of their newness, very little marketing data may be available. In spite of this shortcoming, some honest attempt still has to be made to guesstimate the potential of the product.

Preparing guesstimates may involve telephone interviews or visits to potential users or consumers. It may be necessary to supply samples of the product or equipment either free or at nominal cost to customers, in return for their comments.

There are two ways of conducting market research--by going to an outside market research firm--or attempting to do it internally. The outside firm is likely to charge big dollars. For example attitude studies using focus groups can cost anywhere from $2,000 to $30,000.

A word of caution should be added. Relying on outside market survey expertise can lay a new product open to erroneous conclusions.

A survey conducted many years ago on the potential for the pocket calculator came to the conclusion that the only place for a calculator was on a desk and nobody in their right mind would want to carry one in their pocket, purse or briefcase!

Maybe it is better if the entrepreneur prepares his own survey based on his gut feelings! At least he will have the satisfaction of floating or sinking his own ship, rather than have somebody else do it for him!

The challenge, with the do-it-yourself survey is to remain objective to the realities of the marketplace. Many entrepreneurs fall in love with their new inventions and are blind to consumers who say: "very interesting, but I certainly wouldn't buy it".

Also, conducting market research using internal resources is often hampered by limited manpower and facilities. On the plus side, the costs can be quite modest.

One way is to use students during their summer vacations. For example, they could be used to conduct telephone surveys; assist with direct mailings; conduct on-sight interviews or gather statistics.

What Your Market Survey Should Tell You

A good marketing survey should provide you with information about four things.

Firstly, it should identify the customer profile. It should classify those groups of individuals or companies who either are already purchasing, or will be potential purchasers, of the product or service.

Secondly, it is necessary to identify the total size of the market based on this customer profile.

If your product or service has export potential, then you may want to calculate the market in the United States, which as a rule of thumb, is usually taken at ten times the size of the Canadian market and conversely, for Americans looking north, the Canadian market is about one tenth of the size of the U.S. market.

Information about overseas markets may be more difficult to come by. In this regard, federal, state and provincial governments maintain a number of trade missions overseas. Foreign governments frequently have trade offices in major cities, however, most of these are geared to help promote the products products from their countries, rather than the reverse and some discretion will be called for when requesting information.

31

Thirdly, the market survey should tell you whether the whole market is expanding or contracting. If only parts of it are growing; which parts are they and by how much are they growing?

The market survey should indicate the actual and expected penetrations into the total market. Find out what your market share is now and what you expect it to be in the future.

In the case of new products or services, some idea of rates of growth of market share can be obtained by studying one's competitors or by looking at products or services with similar characteristics; see how long it took to penetrate a certain percentage of the market.

Another way of calculating market penetration, is to conduct telephone or mail surveys of potential users. Yet another, way would be through the test marketing of a product or service; by offering it on a limited basis to a small community of potential users.

Sources of Marketing Information

In the following text, we will look at some of the more common sources of information that you can use when trying to find out more about the market for a product or service.

U.S. Bureau of the Census

Statistical Abstract of the United States:
Public Information Office,
U.S. Bureau of the Census,
U.S. Department of Commerce,
Washington, D.C. 20233
Phone: (301) 457-4608 Fax: (301) 457-4784
Web address: www.census.gov

Statistics Canada

Statistics Canada is Canada's national statistical agency. It collects data and charts the economic, social and social cultural trends of the nation. Data is available to the business community in various formats, including a new on-line service which features a daily news bulletin with summaries of newly released data.

Further information can be obtained from local Statistics Canada Regional Offices by phone, toll-free: 1-(800) 263-1136.

The Ontario Regional Office (Toronto) also offers special Client Services including **Research Service, Priority Telephone Service, Standing Order Service, Special Retrievals** and **Statistical Reports**. Other services include consultations, workshops and custom retrievals. Contact can be made toll-free at the above number or direct by phone at:(416) 973-6586 or by fax at: (416) 973-7475.

Thomas Publishing Co.

Thomas Register: 34 volumes listing 155,000 US and Canadian companies together with their products and services.

American Export Register: lists the products and services of 45,000 U.S. firms.

Thomas Publishing Co.,
Five Penn Plaza, New York City, NY 10001
Phone: (212) 290-7277   Fax: (212) 290-7365

The Alliance of Manufacturers and Exporters

The Canadian Trade Index, 1998 Edition: a four-volume series which lists about 26,000 Canadian companies and 60,000 contacts. It is also available on CD-ROM.

The Alliance of Manufacturers and Exporters
75 International Blvd., 4th Fl., Toronto, ON M9W 6L9
Phone: (416) 798-8000 Ext. 244   Fax: (416) 798-1627

Fraser's Canadian Trade Directory

Fraser's Canadian Trade Directory: List of 35,000 Canadian suppliers, 21,000 product headings and 13,000 registered trade marks. Published in four volumes.

Fraser's Canadian Trade Directory,
777 Bay St., Toronto, ON M5W 1A7
Phone: (416) 596-5086   Fax: (416) 593-3201

Scott's Directories

Scott's Industrial Directories: comprises four directories listing manufacturers in Ontario and Québec. The directories for Western and Atlantic Canada cover both industrial and manufacturing companies. All are now available on computer disk and on CD-ROM. In the disk form, separate industrial disks are available for Ontario and Québec.

National Manufacturers Selectory: a national database of approximately 55,700 Canadian companies and 117,500 executives available on diskette or CD-ROM.

Greater Toronto Business Directory: published in two volumes -Metro and outer boundary. Key information on 31,000 companies including service companies. Both volumes are available on CD ROM or disk.

US Manufacturing Directories: published by Harris Publishing are also distributed in Canada by Scott's Directories.

Scott's Directories,
Southam Business Communications,
1450 Don Mills Rd., Don Mills, ON M3B 2X7
Phone: (416) 442-2122   Fax: (416) 442-2191

Cambridge Information Group

Findex: provides abstracts of about 18,000 market research studies already conducted throughout the world. The abstracts are available in hard copy print; CD-ROM; through the Internet on their WEB site and directly online through "Dialog". Reports can then be obtained directly from the publishers in question.

Cambridge Information Group,
7200 Wisconsin Ave., Suite 601,
Bethesda, Maryland 20814
Phone: (301) 961-6700   Fax: (301) 961-6720
Toll free: 1-(800) 843-7751   Web site: www.csa.com

Information Intelligence Inc.

Online Hotline News Service: produced on CD-ROM, it provides an up-to-date 10-year record of the online and CD-ROM fields. It comprises two components:

Online Newsletter: covers worldwide developments concerning CD-ROM and online.

Online Libraries and Microcomputers: a newsletter on library and information centre developments and applications in North America.

Information Intelligence Inc.,
P.O. Box 31098, Phoenix, Arizona 85046
Phone: (602) 996-2283   E-mail: order@infointelligence.com
Web site: www.infointelligence.com/www/iii-info

The PRS Group

Market Europe, Market Asia Pacific, Market Latin America and Market Africa/Mid-East: monthly marketing journals with a "Quick Query" service for market research information.

The PRS Group,
6320 Sly Rd., #102, P.O. Box 248,
East Syracuse, NY 13057-0248
Web site: www.prsgroup.com
Phone: (315) 431-0511   Fax: (315) 431-0200

Gale Research Inc.

Encyclopedia of Business Information Sources: a directory containing 1,000 sources of American business information.

Consultants and Consulting Organizations Directory: lists 16,557 firms and individuals in US.

Business Organizations, Agencies, and Publications Directory: 23,000 entries on 39 types of business sources.

Gale Directory of Databases: two volumes of current information on 8,500 world-wide databases (on-line, computer-readable and portable), 3,000 producers and 1,600 vendors.

Miscellaneous Directories: company and product information; associations, agencies, research centres; business information; media and publishing; contact books and general reference.

Gale Research Inc.,
835 Penobscot Bldg, Detroit, MI 48226
Phone: (313) 961-2242   Fax: (313) 961-6083
Toll-free fax: 1-(800) 877-4253   Web site: www.gale.com

IntelliSearch

IntelliSearch: provides intelligence on companies worldwide, market research on consumer and industrial products, subject searches in journal articles, patents and trade marks. IntelliSearch staff can perform searches on a fee-for-service basis and have access to over 1.5 million books, 450 commercial online databases, 600 business directories, 6000 periodical and magazine subscriptions, 250 newspaper titles, the Internet and the World Wide Web, telephone and city directories from all over the world, Statistics Canada and federal government documents, filings of the Ontario Securities Commission and the U.S. Securities and Exchange Commission.

IntelliSearch,
Metropolitan Toronto Reference Library,
789 Yonge St., Toronto, ON M4W 2G8
Phone: (416) 393-7241   Fax: (416) 393-7169
E-mail: intellisearch@mtrl.toronto.on.ca

Online Search Service

Online Search Service of the North York Public Library: databases of literature, books, business directories, encyclopedias, conference reports, government documents, trademarks, patents.

Online Search Service, Electronic Resources,
3rd. Floor, North York Public Library,
5120 Yonge St., North York,
ON M2N 5N9
Phone: (416) 395-5579 Fax (416) 395-5669

Market Statistics

Demographics USA: provides market statistics in three volumes: by county, city and zip code.

Market Statistics,
355 Park Avenue South,
New York, NY 10010
Phone: (212) 592-6244   Fax: (212) 592-6259
Web site: www.marketstats.com

The Financial Post DataGroup

Canadian Markets: comprises data based on Statistics Canada reports which profiles over 700 urban markets in Canada; the people of Canada; their spending habits; housing; families; income; level of schooling; occupations; travel statistics; retail sales; taxation etc. It is available in both printed format and CD-ROM.

The Financial Post DataGroup,
333 King St. E.,
Toronto, ON M5A 4N2
Phone: (416) 350-6507   Fax: (416) 350-6501
Toll free: 1-(800) 661-7678
E-mail: fpdg@fpdata.finpost.com

Dun and Bradstreet

DMI - Dun's Market Identifiers: provides access to a massive database covering 1.1 million Canadian businesses. Also available online on Dialog and Informant.

Guide to Canadian Manufacturers: lists 10,000 top manufacturers.

Canadian Key Business Directory: provides data on 20,000 top businesses together with 100,000 key employees.

Regional Services Directory: lists the top 20,000 business service companies in Canada.

National Services Directory: lists 12,000 services throughout Canada.

Dun and Bradstreet Canada Limited,
Marketing Services Division,
5770 Hurontario, Mississauga, ON   L5R 3G5
Phone: (905) 568-6000 or toll free: 1-(800)-INFO-DNB
Fax: (905) 568-6073

IHS/Micromedia Limited

Associations Canada: The Directory of Associations in Canada describes 20,000 Canadian associations with 3,000 subject headings. It is also available on CD ROM.

CREDO: Canadian Research and Electronic Documents Ordering provides indexing on company filings with the Ontario Security Commission as well as government and research documents. It also comprises a document ordering facility.

Profile Canada: a marketing database covering 25,000 Canadian companies and organizations. Also available on CD-ROM.

Directory of Libraries in Canada: lists 6,500 libraries and is also available on CD ROM.

Canadian Almanac & Directory: fully indexed information on Canadian culture, financial and government institutions, legislative, judicial and education systems. Also on CD-ROM.

Canadian Environmental Directory: information on government agencies, associations, consulting firms and educational establishments involved in environmental-related activities.

Financial Services Canada Directory: fully indexed directory of Canadian financial institutions and organizations.

IHS/Micromedia Limited, 20 Victoria St.,
Toronto, Ont. M5C 2N8   Toll free: 1-(800) 387-2689
Phone: (416) 362-5211   Fax: (416) 362-6161
E-mail: info@micromedia.on.ca
Web site: www.micromedia.on.ca

Industry Canada

Canadian Company Capabilities (CCC): an online multi-media database which profiles 32,000 Canadian companies and their products, services or operations.

Strategic Information Branch, Industry Canada,
235 Queen St., Ottawa ON K1A 0H5
Phone: 1-(800) 328-6189   Fax: (613) 954-1894
E-mail: hotline.service@ic.gc.ca
Web site: http://strategis.ic.gc.ca

Bowker-Saur, K.G. Saur

Directory of European Business: lists 4,000 businesses and 12,000 contacts in 33 European countries.

Online/CD-ROM Business Sourcebook: lists the most important electronic databases worldwide.

European R&D Database on CD-ROM: profiles over 21,000 research facilities and 85,000 senior researchers in 34 different Western and Eastern European countries.

Yearbook of International Organizations: provides information on over 30,000 organizations in over 300 countries.

The SBS World Guide: fact files on every country of the world including historical reviews, current government, population, economy, international relations, communications, geography and maps.

Bowker-Saur, K.G. Saur, 121 Chanlon Rd.,
New Providence, NJ 07974
Order Phone: 1-888-BOWKER2
Order Fax: 1-908-506-7696
E-Mail info@bowker.com
Web Page: http://www.bowker.com

MRCA Information Services

National Consumer Panel Database: monitors consumer purchasing of packaged soft goods (apparel, home furnishing and footwear) products.

Packaged Goods and Products Database: covers preparation and consumption of packaged goods and products.

MRCA Information Services,
20 Summer St., Stamford, CONN. 06901
Phone: (203) 324-9600   Fax: (203) 348-4087

The UnCover Company

The UnCover Company: an on-line periodical article delivery service providing open access to more than 8 million articles in 17,000 journals worldwide.

SOS - Single Order Force: which allows those without computers to access articles.

Reveal - which is a table of contents alerting system which permits up to 50 journal titles and 25 keyboard searches.

The UnCover Company, c/o CARL Corporation,
3801 E. Florida Ave., Suite 300, Denver CO 80210
Phone: (303) 758-3030   Fax: (303) 758-5946
Web site: http://uncweb.carl.org

Reed-Elsevier

Yearbook of International Organizations: lists 28,000 organizations in 200 countries. Also on CD-ROM.

Directory of American Research and Technology: lists over 11,000 U.S. and Canadian corporate facilities active in basic and applied research.

Standard Directory of Advertising Agencies: profiles 8,700 top US advertising agencies and their branches in the US and abroad.

Direct Marketing Marketplace: lists 4,720 direct marketing companies 3,500 service firms and suppliers in the US.

Information Source and Other Directories: show where to get information. There is also a directory of books in print.

America's Corporate Finance Directory: profiles 5,000 leading public and private companies in the USA, 18,000 subsidiaries and 31,000 outside service firms.

Directory of Corporate Affiliations: lists 117,000 of the world's leading companies and 286,000 key executives.

Reed-Elsevier, 121 Chanlon Rd.,
New Providence, NJ 07974
Toll free: 1-(800) 521-8110   Web site: www.reedref.com
Phone: (908) 464-6800   Fax: (908) 665-6688

Angus Reid Group

Angus Reid Group: a Canadian market/social research and polling company providing information and advice. It has offices in nine major cities in the USA and Canada, together with an associate in Mexico and alliances around the world. It offers a **World Monitor Service** in conjunction with The Globe and Mail, The Economist and CTV.

Angus Reid Group,
One Nicholas St., Suite 1400,
Ottawa, ON K1N 7B7
Phone: (613) 241-5802   Fax: (613) 241-5460

Public Libraries

Many of the directories mentioned above can be found in the business sections of public libraries.

Trade Associations

Trade associations in North America can be an invaluable source of information about the industries or sectors which they represent.

Trade Magazines

Trade journals and magazines - Canadian, American and European - can be found covering most industries and services. These were covered earlier in this book.

Get to Know Your Competition!

Before you can come up with a marketing strategy, it is essential that you study your competition. Get hold of their advertising brochures and catalogues. Visit their web site. Find out who they are and how much of the market they control. Examine their marketing and advertising strategies.

Develop Your Marketing Strategy

Your study of your potential market should allow you to identify your prime prospects in the form of potential end users of your product or service. Thus, your market survey provides a firm foundation upon which to build a marketing strategy.

The objective of developing such a strategy is to position your business in such a way as to gain a competitive advantage in the marketplace.

YOU NEED TO GET THE RIGHT PRODUCT IN THE RIGHT MARKET AT THE RIGHT TIME WITH THE RIGHT PRICE..

A marketing strategy is very similar in essence to military strategy. The business owner (the general) is attempting to defeat the competition (the enemy) by the correct positioning of his product or service (his troops).

Now, in business as in battle, there are winners and losers. Just as in battle, the chances of winning are enhanced by knowing your own strengths and weaknesses, as well as those of your opponents (the competition). Taking advantage of the weaknesses of your opponents, means correctly positioning your product in the marketplace.

5

PLANNING YOUR BUSINESS

Why You Need A Plan

The importance of having a good business plan cannot be overemphasized. It is almost universally asked for by bankers, venture capitalists or potential investors in your business. In addition, it forces you to think through your strategy and set proper and realistic objectives.

A plan shows that you have addressed yourself to the key elements of your business. It helps you lay down on paper where you intend to go and how you propose to get there.

You can have an accountant or business consultant prepare your plan. Expect to pay anywhere from $3,000 to $5,000 and possibly a lot more, if you are using a big name firm.

If the prospect of selling "Old Betsy", the faithful family car, to raise the money for preparing the plan appals you, remember that you can always do it yourself.

A good plan is not something that can be rushed off in a couple of hours. It may take ten days, working full-time to prepare a good brief. Ideally, it should be 20-50 pages in length. It should be thorough and cover all the relevant aspects of your business.

Business Planning Software

Knowing how to use spreadsheet software will greatly assist you in all aspects of your business planning and I would strongly recommend you to learn one of the popular programs before embarking on your business venture. The three most popular software packages are: *Lotus, 1,2,3*; *Excel* and *Quattro Pro*. All of them will allow you to analyze the performance of your business; calculate your gross margins by product line; analyze the effectiveness of your direct marketing campaigns etc. The only challenge is that you will have to set these up for yourself.

Many of the major banks offer free business planning software for their business customers. Even if you don't use it, I would still advise you to get a copy, just to get a feel for how to go about preparing the document.

In addition, there are commercial packages available for preparing business plans, Many of these are covered in more detail in my book (also published by Productive Publications) called: *Software for Small Business: 1999 Edition - A Review of the Latest Windows Programs to Help You Improve Business Efficiency and Productivity (Using Windows 95 and Windows 98)*.

Setting Objectives

To be effective, strategic objectives must be clearly defined and then given a time frame. There should be near-term, medium-term and long-term objectives. This is another way of asking the following questions: where do you want the company to be 12 months from now? where do you want it to be 3-5 years from now? where would you like to have steered it 10-20 years from now?

The asking of basic, key questions is the essence in art of planning. Such questions are often of the nature: "Where do we want to be 12 months from now. How are we going to get there?" The answers become the basis for setting strategic objectives.

The goals will vary from business to business and from circumstance to circumstance, but without exception involve growing the business and taking it to a higher level of sales and profitability.

Make sure that the objectives are realistic. As a consultant, I have seen many entrepreneurs present me with "pie-in-the-sky" objectives that were completely unrealistic. It's all very well to set an objective for let's say, $10 million of sales in the next twelve months. Many questions arise: does the company have the resources? has it got the money to do it?

There are also the questions: is there sufficient market to absorb the product or service? is the competition going to play dead?

One of the first considerations in assessing the realism of objectives is to examine the time frame. The objective of $10 million in sales in five years **may be** very attainable - but it **may not be** within a short twelve month time frame.

There is little substitute for experience and market knowledge in the area of setting realistic objectives. Most objectives take much longer to reach than was thought when they were formulated.

Another way of looking at it, is to work back from the objective e.g., a goal of $12 million in sales within twelve months - and examine all the bits and pieces that would have to be put in place, month by month in order to achieve that objective.

Let's say that you are manufacturing widgets and that you sell them for $10.00 each. That means that you would need to produce a million widgets in the next twelve months. Let's say that it will take you three months to find a location, get all the equipment in place and train staff. It might take another three months to get a sales force and distribution network set up, which leaves six months to produce and sell a million widgets. Look at it another way: this means producing and selling 200,000 widgets a month - or about 50,000 per week - or about 10,000 per day. Now, if your machinery only makes 100 per day you're in big trouble!!

Obviously, the above is an extremely ridiculous example, but it serves to illustrate the kind of thinking that you should go through when determining if your objectives are realistic or not.

Much harm can be done if the company gears up production only to find that the market will not absorb its output or the company does not have the distribution power to sell it to the market. In fact, such an event could spell disaster.

You have to ask yourself: "What is the competition going to do?" It is unlikely that they will throw up their arms in open welcome. They may cut prices or take defensive strategies to preserve their market share.

52

You also have to ask yourself if there are there any real benefits to be attained as a result of following certain objectives? Thus, if the goal is to double sales - will this result in a doubling of profit? Or, will the costs associated with obtaining those extra sales be greater than they are worth and actually lead to a decline in profits?

If an objective involves the purchase of a piece of equipment, you should ask the question: " will there be any cost benefit to the business? How long will it be before the equipment is paid off? Will the equipment sing for its supper?"

For instance, if a start-up company engaged in manufacturing has decided to purchase an expensive die-cutting machine - will the machine pay for itself? Or, would it be cheaper to sub-contract the work to somebody who has the equipment? What would happen if that other "somebody" went out of business? What is the likelihood of this happening? Key questions have to be asked when you are setting objectives and defining the future direction for your business.

You also have to ask yourself if there are too many objectives. Will the business be going off in too many directions at once and end up spreading itself so thin, that one crack with a baseball bat will shatter the whole thing? As a consultant, I have seen this so many times. Some entrepreneurs in their enthusiasm to grow big as fast as possible, set off in many different directions at once with the end-result that they get nowhere. The key is to remain focussed. By all means, "tweak" your objectives and add things or subtract things, but only if they help you attain your ultimate objectives.

Some of the best objectives are those in which maybe only one, or at the most two, long term goals are identified. Other objectives can be added so as to provide stepping-stones to that ultimate objective. In other words, the company progresses along a path from objective-to-objective.

You should also be prepared to alter your objectives in response to changes.

When planning, you should take into account the possibilities of something unexpected happening. For instance, the owner, who has been healthy all his life, suddenly has a heart attack. Can somebody run the business in the owner's absence? If the general gets shot will there be a brigadier or colonel to take his place?

Sudden change is difficult to monitor. It either happens or it doesn't!

Gradual change, on the other hand, can and should be monitored. Such changes are likely to have an effect on the objectives that have been set. If these objectives are rigid and hewn in stone, then they may prove to be unattainable. To put it another way, it is no use shooting in the same direction after somebody has moved the target!

Responding to change is a little like shooting at a moving target. The gun sights have to be constantly altered to account for different distances and the direction the gun is pointing also has to be altered.

Change may make the objective closer or (as is normally the case) further, in the time horizon. The direction of thrust may have to be changed as the business goal changes. If the target or objective disappears altogether, then it is time to sit down and think the whole thing through again!

All that has been said thus far is of no use unless changes are monitored and plans are altered or modified in response to them. It's a good idea to sit down every few months and see how you are doing in relation to the objectives that you have established.

Change is not bad. If it was not for change, many opportunities would not present themselves. Taking advantage of change can present enormous potential possibilities for growth.

Take the typewriter as an example. The manual version was replaced by the electric. The electric was then replaced by the electronic. In turn, the electronic has now been replaced by the computer using word processing software in conjunction with a laser or ink-jet printer.

In trying to attain your objectives, it does not matter how many times the plan has to be altered - the main thing is to get there. Tenzing and Hillary knew their objective was to to be the first to climb Mount Everest. They had planned their route but they still had to make little detours as they approached their objective. (AND THEY HAD ONLY TWO OBJECTIVES - REACH THE TOP AND GET BACK DOWN SAFELY!)

Put in a nutshell, you must have only a few realistic objectives and be prepared to modify them in the light of emerging realities.

Put Your Objectives Into A Time Frame

Your objectives should consider where you would like be one year from now; five years from now and over a longer time span. Divide them into three sections.

Immediate Objectives: some realistic objectives that you feel that you can comfortably meet in the next twelve months. Examples might be, the completion of certain prototypes; completion of product packaging design; setting up of X number of sales agents; sales volume targets etc.

Intermediate Objectives: should outline where you would like to be five years from now (aside from sitting on your private yacht in the Adriatic!)? Into what new markets might you consider expanding? Will you start developing any new products or variations to your existing product line?

Longer Term Objectives: should define your place in your industry group. What will you be doing about expanding into international markets., etc.

Once you have divided your objectives up into immediate, intermediate and long term, you are ready to put them into a time frame. This gives some teeth to your objectives, especially in the immediate term. Put down the dates when you hope to achieve certain things. Objectives really don't mean much unless you can put some dates to them.

Will the Business Make Money

This is a very obvious question, however, as a consultant, I have seen so many people dive into business without giving it much serious consideration.

You see people rushing out to open a small retail store and because they cannot afford outside staff, they end up working 12 hours a day, six days a week, fifty-two weeks a year only to find that they are making less than minimum wage. Is it worth it?

I know it is hard to predict what the future holds financially, but there is a way if you are willing to take the time to prepare cash flow statements and cash flow projections. We'll discuss them in the next section.

Cash Flow: The Life Blood of Every Business

Once you have established your objectives, it's time to determine how much money will be required to achieve those objectives. In arriving at the amount, you will first need to prepare a set of sales projections - how much of the product or service you feel that you can reasonably produce or supply each month for the first year, the second year, etc.

If you are involved in manufacturing, you will have to figure out your unit costs - how much it costs to produce each widget. Will the costs become less; the higher the volume and if so, by how much?

In the case of a service company, such as a window cleaning service, figure out how much it costs to clean each window (labour cost, gas for vehicle, detergent etc.).

Then you will need to figure out your capital costs. Find out what equipment you will need to produce the high tech mouse trap and how much it costs. In the case of service companies, the equipment requirement may cost much less - vehicle, bucket, squeegee, ladder, rope!

Next, you will have to figure out your overhead - what will the rent be for manufacturing space and office space, together with such things as heat, light, water, telephone etc. Calculate this on a monthly basis.

How many people will you require and what will you have to pay them? Don't forget the "hidden" costs, such as: vacation pay, workman's compensation, allowance for sick leave, pension plan contributions, health insurance, employment insurance, etc.

What are your selling or distribution costs going to be? Are you going to sell by direct mail, at trade shows? How much will you have to allow for advertising and promotional costs? Are you going to use the yellow pages, newspapers, magazines etc?

How much inventory will you require? This is particularly important for people in retail or manufacturing. How much money is going to be tied up on the shelves on a monthly basis?

Make allowance for taxes - especially municipal and corporate. The cost of collecting sales taxes should be taken into account.

After all this calculating, you will be able to come up with a cash flow projection that will enable you to identify how much money you really need. This will also indicate whether the business will fly from a financial viewpoint.

The best way to envisage cash flow is to envisage a bath tub with one tap in and one drain out.

Imagine the tap is fully open and water (cash from sales or the money which was put into the business) is rushing into the tub. Then, imagine that the outflow drain plug is only partly in place. The water that is flowing out represents the money that is being spent on capital equipment, overhead, wages, inventory etc. - it has gone.

The water that is left in the tub (if any!) represents the money that remains in the bank which can wither be used to expand the business, pay off debt or is available to be taken out by the owner.

However, if the water is flowing out of the tub faster than it is coming in, the tub (bank account) will be empty and the owner will not have any money to take out for him or herself.

Change the design of the tub a bit! Let us say that there are two taps providing water. The "capital tap" provides the start-up capital from the entrepreneur or in the case of a lender, it is called the "loan tap". It may also be a combination of them.

The other tap (let's call it the "sales revenue tap") keeps bringing water into the tub, but the sum total of the water from both taps must be greater than the amount of water flowing out of the tub or the business will be in trouble. The owner won't have any money to pay him or herself and will have to cut back on the amount of money flowing out of the tub to stop the business from being forced to close.

In a very simplistic way, this is the basis of cash flow. Cash inflow includes revenue from sales, start-up money, loans, etc., and cash outflow includes expenses, interest on the loan, loan repayments, taxes, etc. It should be noted that the concept of cash flow does not make allowance for the depreciation of capital assets, such as equipment, vehicles or real estate

In preparing a cash flow statement, you divide time up into months, quarters (3-month periods January 1st to March 31st, April 1st to June 30th, July 1st to September 30th and October 1st to December 31st) or years (which can be a calendar year January 1st to December 31st or fiscal year which usually starts at the beginning of a specific month and ends twelve months later.

So, going back to our bath tub analogy, let's say that you have twelve tubs in a row, starting on the left with a tub called "January", the next one is "February" and so on. If there is still some water in the January tub at the end of the month, this will be removed and put into (carried forward to) the February tub, right at the beginning of the month.

Whilst the above analogy represents a simplification of the concept of cash flow, it still illustrates how vital it is to the survival of the business. It also demonstrates the need for the injection of cash or seed capital to get the business going. Let's abandon the bath tubs and examine an initial two month period:

MONTH ONE

```
CASH BALANCE AT BEGINNING                    $0
ADD CASH COMING IN:
Cash from entrepreneur     25,000
Cash from sales                 0
Total cash coming in:                    25,000
TOTAL CASH AVAILABLE                     25,000

LESS CASH GOING OUT:
Machinery purchase         10,000
Rent                        1,000
Office supplies               100
Telephone & answering         100
Inventory                   5,000
Wages                       4,000
Selling & advertising       1,800
Total cash going out:                    22,000

CASH BALANCE AT END                       3,000
```

MONTH TWO

```
CASH BALANCE AT BEGINNING
(carried forward)                        3,000
ADD CASH COMING IN:
Cash from entrepreneur          0
Cash from sales             3,000
Total cash coming in:                    3,000

TOTAL CASH AVAILABLE                     6,000

LESS CASH GOING OUT:
Rent                        1,000
Office supplies               100
Telephone & answering         100
Inventory                   1,000
Wages                       4,000
Production/selling costs    1,800
Total cash going out:                    8,000

CASH DEFICIENCY AT END                  (2,000)
```

Let's examine this example in a little more detail.

The business is actually making $2,200 (3,000 - 1,800) on its sales, however, when overhead (rent, office supplies, telephone) are taken away, together with the costs of purchasing more inventory and wages we actually end up with a cash deficiency of $5,000. However, there was $3,000 brought forward from the first month, so the cash deficiency is reduced to $2,000.

Where is this money going to come from to cover the deficiency? Are wages going to be cut back, is more product going to be sold, will the price of the product have to be increased or will the entrepreneur have to put more money into the business?

What happens if he does not have any more money? Maybe it can be borrowed or maybe an investor can be found. By that stage it may be too late - the employees have quit when they didn't receive their pay cheques!

The time to find all this out is in advance. Create cash flow models, such as this and keep repeating until you find out if the project will fly on its own with your own money or if you will have to go outside to look for cash. The exercise will also allow you to obtain an idea of how much you realistically require to put the show on the road.

It must be recognized that the above discussion is very much simplified. Things like trade credit can affect the figures quite dramatically.

For entrepreneurs going into manufacturing, their customers may demand payment terms of 30 days, which in reality, usually means you may not receive your money for 60 days or more, depending on how good you are at getting your customers to pay up. (As a consultant, I am constantly amazed at how many cash flow projections I have seen that do not take this into account.)

On the other hand, your suppliers may not be willing to offer you credit because you are new in business and represent too high a risk for them.

If you think about this for a moment, you will notice that your money is coming in much slower than it is going out. This is quite typical for a company in start-up mode.

62

Taking the figures we used above, if trade terms of 30 days were offered on sales of product and assuming that, in practice the money is not received until 60 days later, this means that the cash would not be received until the third month. The company would then have a cash deficiency of $5,000.00 in the second month.

What Will it Cost to Get Started?

In the course of my consulting work, I have come across many cases where the need has not been properly established. "We'll need $100,000 ....we need $60,000 ....we need $250,000."

Closer examination often reveals that the amounts sought are either too high or too low. More frequently than not, they are too low. New business owners don't allow for the delay in receiving payments for goods shipped. They don't allow for the true costs of overhead. In addition, estimated production costs are frequently too low.

The most common mistake is to assume that sales will take off immediately.

Customers are often reluctant to try a new product. They stall: "Great widget - but I'll have to think about it!" ..."Good idea this window washing service - but I'll have to talk to the wife about it!"

It's a rare product where customers beat a path to the door of those who are producing it! Make allowance for this in your cash flow planning! Make sure that you are going to have enough cash to keep the company afloat until your market is properly developed and incorporate this into your strategic planning.

The most obvious question relating to the requirement for starting-up a business is what is the minimum amount of money required?

Once you have established the minimum, you can put in extras for contingencies. Here, it is best to over-estimate the amount needed. Peter A Cortese, President of Alpha Systems once said: "Whatever you think it is going to take, double it".

The next factor is to decide how long you need the money for. This, in turn, will depend on your projections on the length of time it will take to reap the financial rewards from achieving your strategic objective.

How soon is the money going to be required? For many entrepreneurs, it was yesterday! For others, the requirement may lie sometime in the future.

From a cynical viewpoint, it can be argued that the best time to obtain money is when you least need it! When you are doing well, the money will come chasing after you. This is especially true of bank financing.

We will cover financing in more detail later in this book. The point that we want to make here is that cash flow projections will help you to determine your financing requirements. More importantly, they will help you determine if your business is going to make any money.

Detailed Planning Depends on the Type of Business

You will probably have noticed that this chapter has been short on specifics when it comes to preparing a business plan. That was done on purpose, because detailed planning depends upon the type of business you want to operate.

The following chapters will look at some of the more common types of businesses and point out some of the factors that you need to consider when doing your planning.

64

6

LOCATION, LOCATION, LOCATION

The Significance of Location

The best location for your business is highly dependent upon the type of activities that you're engaged in.

A number of years ago a well-known business person (and for the life of me, I cannot remember his name), stated that the three most important things to remember when starting a business are: location, location, location. This is certainly true for a great many businesses, however, the importance of location is diminishing in the case of certain types of businesses involved with the new economy. To consider this in more detail, let us examine a number of different types of businesses and the importance that location plays for them.

In the case of retail stores, location is of paramount importance because you need to be able to attract customers to visit your location. Again, this can vary according to the type of retail business. Many shops are located along streets or there is a good flow of pedestrian traffic that will browse in windows and hopefully enter the store to make a purchase. The same is true of shops that are located in strip malls or shopping plazas which rely on the traffic generated by the "anchor stores" (usually major department stores, grocery chains, liquor stores or Post Offices).

It is only the deep discount stores (such as Costco/Price Club) that can induce people to drive to the perimeter of a city or town to make their purchase.

In the case of manufacturing plants, most are restricted by city bylaws to certain specific areas. In addition to this, an entrepreneur who is considering going into manufacturing should consider the local pool of labor, ready access to suppliers, access to customers (if that is a factor), access to railway lines (if that is needed) or, the need to be located near to an airport, if frequent air travel is a factor. The owner should also consider the amount of time that it takes for him or her to commute to the business location. It is pointless locating a business in a location that takes hours to reach in the rush-hour.

The best location for companies involved in the service areas will depend upon the service being offered. Once again, they should be located close to their customers. This is particularly true for people in the food service business who need to locate their restaurant or snack bar in a place which is easy to reach and has high visibility to attract walk-in customers. On the other hand, a business involved with washing windows will not require a high visibility location since all the work is conducted at the customer's location. The same holds true for the businesses of most trades people, such as plumbers, electricians, people involved with landscaping, etc.

Other businesses which offer a service such as, dentists, doctors, accountants, lawyers, etc., are best advised to locate their businesses in locations which are easily accessible by their patients or clients. In certain cases, some law firms or accountants might want to locate in prestigious buildings in order to create the image which they feel is appropriate to their business. For others, this may not be so important, however, would you want to visit a dentist located in a rundown shack?

As mentioned above, the new economy is changing the importance of location for businesses. Thus, many businesses can be operated out of the owner's home and indeed this is a great way to keep costs and minimum during the early stages of business growth. Most home-based businesses can disguise the fact that they are located at home through the use of private mailbox of services of which they are a number of franchises, such as Mail Boxes Etc., which allow you to use a street address for your mail and parcels to be delivered.

When establishing a home-based business, care should be taken not to violate local bylaws. In practice, you will find that most municipalities are fairly tolerant of home-based businesses provided that they are not engaged in retail or service businesses which necessitate a lot of people coming and going. In addition, most municipalities will not allow you to post any signs in front of your dwelling to indicate that it is a business location.

As mentioned in an earlier chapter, the home-based business can allow you some generous write-offs from a tax viewpoint. Most home-based business owners can use as an expense for tax purposes a portion of the rent or mortgage payment that is directly related to the portion of the dwelling that is used supposedly for business purposes.

In addition, the home-based business owner does not have to waste a lot of time commuting to and from work. Thus, many people in a major city such as Toronto, Chicago or Los Angeles can spend at least an hour or more getting to work and the same again into the evening. If you work this out, this amounts to 10 hours or more of time wasted every week which is equivalent to about 500 hours per year. If you are awake for average of 16 hours per day, you can easily calculate that you will waste a full month every year just getting to and from work!

Internet-based businesses have a lot in common with home-based businesses. Indeed, many are operated from a home or from a low rent location with little or no visibility required from pedestrian traffic. Indeed, many of the employees can also work from home since those involved with accounting and sales can perform these functions just as well at home now that we have low telecommunication costs and powerful computer networks ("extranets") which allow employees access to any critical company information they need in order to carry on their work.

Businesses that sell direct to the consumer through a catalogue, by direct mail or through telemarketing also do require prestigious, high rent locations.

I already know of one organization located in British Columbia, which has a mandate to assist women entrepreneurs and maintains a "virtual office" with no one physical location; the "locations" being determined by where the employees are in their homes or cottages at any given time.

The last type of business that we will consider here is one whose location is constantly changing Thus, an ice cream van, or hot dog vendor conducts his or her business at the location of their van or cart. In reality, however, such business people still have location where they keep their financial records, supplies, etc., in addition to providing a location to park their van or cart when they are not actively in use.

Cost Benefits of the Location

High traffic retail locations carry with them higher rents and the business owner has to make a decision as to whether the higher rents will offset the increased traffic. The same holds true for businesses which for one reason or another, have to be located in the downtown core of a major city.

As a consultant, I remember one case in particular where the owner of an audio-visual rental business was forced to vacate his downtown premises because the landlord wanted to sell it to a developer. Unfortunately, this happened at a time of exceptionally high rents for business space near the downtown core. However, he was able to find some space not to far away, which served his purpose.

In an effort to avoid a repeat performance of what he had just been through, he had his lawyer draw up a water-tight agreement with the new landlord. Unfortunately, this agreement also denied him any escape from the lease and the rent was so high that he was hard-pressed to make any money. He tried to sell the business, but was unsuccessful and subsequently suffered a heart attack. At that time he was forced into partnership with somebody else, against his wishes, just to keep the business afloat.

In another instance, I know of the owner of a copy shop who was faced with a combined rent and business tax increase of 50%; bringing his total monthly rent to $6,000 - a sum which broke the camel's back and forced him to close down his business.

In yet another instance, I know of a fairly successful restaurant/deli which had operated near a high-traffic intersection for years which was held to ransom by a greedy landlord when it came time for renewal of the lease. In that instance, the restaurant owner simply refused to pay the increase and posted a notice in his window in which he thanked his patrons and stated he was closing down because of the exorbitant rent increase that he was faced with.

Stories like these should alert you to the fact that rent will be one of your major expenses and high rents have to be cost-justified with increased business to be worth while. If the business requires a high traffic location, but cannot generate enough revenue to leave a decent profit after paying the rent, then the business concept should be thought through again to see if a lower cost location may work, and if not, then the idea may need to be abandoned.

What You Will Need If You Are Going Into Manufacturing

Consider the total square footage required for your future plant. Break this down into office space, warehouse facilities, manufacturing facilities. Think about any special features that may be required such as dock-level loading, dust free environment, special heating or cooling, any special water requirements or electrical - do you need 220 volt power?

Find out the going rates for the type of premises you need and use these figures in your projections.

You will also need to consider how long such facilities will be sufficient for your operation? How soon will you have to consider renting additional space? Can you obtain an option on additional space within your building or will you have to move?

Some companies use outside warehousing if their space requirements vary considerably from time-to-time during the year. For example, if your product is oriented towards the Christmas season, your space requirements may be very large in the months leading up to Christmas but very small thereafter. Rather than renting a lot of space you don't need, warehousing may be the answer where you can arrange to pay only for the space your goods occupy.

If your components are imported, you may wish to use bonded warehousing so that you only pay duties when the goods are released through customs as your require them.

What You Will Need If You Are Opening a Retail Store

Of paramount importance is the geographic location. It has to be such as to offer exposure to shoppers who come by foot, or those who use transportation such as automobile or subway. If you are locating on a street with little pedestrian traffic and are relying on passing motorists, you must consider the availability of parking.

When laying out your store, you will need to calculate the square footage that will be used for selling as opposed to stock and administrative space.

Your lease will probably be one of the most important documents that you sign. You have to protect yourself because if you have spent many years building up a loyal customer base, you don't want to suddenly find that your lease is terminated (e.g., if the landlord decides to sell the building for re-development) or that your rents suddenly take an enormous jump in cost when your lease comes up for renewal. Try and sign a lease for as long as you can with renewal options in which the rates of any rent increases are clearly defined.

If you intend to locate in a mall, what percentage of sales do you have to pay to mall management?

I recommend that you seek <u>good</u> legal advice from a lawyer or attorney with experience in this area, before signing any agreement.

What will your maintenance costs be? Are your responsibilities clearly defined in the lease.

Project your future space requirements. If you move, will your customers still patronize your business?

Think about your proposed store layout (with a sketch if possible); the decor; the fixturing and how you intend to display your products. How much will you rely on display lighting? Will you have background music to create a mood and will you use your public address system to announce specials?

What are you going to do about shoplifting and pilferage. Does your layout leave areas of the store hidden where thieves can pocket goods? Consider a display height that always leaves the upper part of customers visible. Will you be installing security cameras and surveillance mirrors?

Shrinkage is no laughing matter. I remember a number of years ago, when I was selling the security surveillance products, talking to the head of security of a drug chain which was experiencing theft at an average of $10,000 per weekend at a downtown location. As a former police officer, he was not prepared to consider cameras, mirrors and a store layout that was not conducive to shoplifting; but rather favored the police approach of "I've got to get my man"and employed undercover floorwakers to catch the thieves. Soon, however, these undercover floorwalkers were spending their entire days in court waiting for their cases to come up and no-one was guarding the store! The pilfering continued and eventually the entire chain closed down and sold out to a competitor. One of the first things the competitor did was to close down the store with the high pilferage.

7

HUMAN RESOURCES

The people who work for you can make you or break you. It is very important right from the start to assemble the best team of people that you can possible afford to run the business. If you cannot afford outside help, then you will have to do all the work yourself or use sub-contractors until you reach the stage at which you can start hiring employees.

In calculating your human resource requirements, you should divide the employees you need into certain broad categories, such as those required for manufacturing, those required in shipping and receiving, those required for order-taking, sales and marketing and those required for accounting and bookkeeping (which could include issuing invoices, collecting money from customers, paying wages, paying bills and calculating taxes). Outline the job descriptions of each employee which you will require and find out what the going wage rates are for each.

Selecting the right people is very important for any manufacturing operation. It is of paramount importance in any service industry because the business is built around its people; not its products.

Since salaries and wages form one of the largest expenses in any service organization, these costs should be considered in detail, together with any incentive schemes.

Training

It's fine to hire people, but if they are not familiar with your particular type of business or the tasks that have to be performed, they will need to be trained. This takes time, money and patience, however, sometimes government assistance is available and you should check this out.

You also have to be prepared for setbacks. Thus, I heard of a case where a company had spent several months training an employee only to have him quit when the training was over!

If you are using tradespeople in your business, such as electricians, plumbers, welders etc., you may want to check out any apprenticeship programs that may be available through your local colleges.

Quality Control

Quality control is an important factor to consider in both manufacturing and service companies. In the case of manufacturing, a number of international standards of quality assurance are starting to emerge such as, ISO, etc. These are particularly important when securing military, government and other contracts and of even greater importance when dealing with overseas companies; especially those in Europe.

Standards for quality control and quality assurance vary from industry to industry and the best place to find out about them is through any trade associations that cover your area or through your local Board of Trade or Chamber of Commerce.

Employee Remuneration

Obviously, you have to pay your employees a fair wage in order to retain them, however, you have to make sure that they are happy and well looked after because in a tight job market they can up and leave at a moment's notice.

Remember, it may take several months to find replacements and train them. This represents time lost in running your business and it is something to bear in mind when you get requests for small pay increases.

Indeed, pay should be reviewed on a periodic basis and employees should be rewarded for good performance.

The advantage that a small business has is that its employees can become part of "the family" and provide a sense of belonging that is not present in large, uncaring operations where employees are treated like cogs in a big machine. It would behoove the small business owner to try and cultivate the "family" atmosphere in the business. It does not cost much to have a picnic outing in the summer or treating employees to a nice dinner at Christmas time can have a big payback in employee loyalty.

The big disadvantage facing small businesses is their inability to offer the same generous benefits packages (such as health insurance, pension plans) as their larger counterparts which can negotiate good deals with insurance and pension plan companies. On the other hand, membership in some trade associations may enable you to obtain good deals because of the negotiating power of the association.

Employee Share Ownership Plans

Could this be a small business owner's dream? Employees who arrive early for work; stay late without demanding overtime; never take sick leave; have perfect quality control and display unnerving loyalty to corporate well-being!

Or, could this be the demented fantasy of a small business owner, after a frustrating day of management by crisis? Maybe it is the latest offering of a steel collar worker from the catalogue of Toshiba's System Robots?

It might be none of these! It could be the product of an ingenious twist of capitalism that places share ownership in the hands of workers.

Employee Share Ownership Plans or "ESOPs" as they are commonly referred to, provide a mechanism whereby employees can participate in the fortunes of the companies for which they work.

There are two aspects to employee participation in the ownership of a business.

The first, is the sense of pride which employees obtain from knowing that they own part of the business. This helps ensure maximum profitability for the firm.

The second aspect is the true financing of the business. This is especially true for early-stage companies, who may not have the cash to pay for high-calibre or skilled employees, but are able to make up part of their wages in the form of stock. This was the case with Apple Computer, when it first started, and resulted in a number of their employees eventually becoming millionaires.

There is also a story about a cleaning lady at Canadian Tire's head office, in Toronto, who joined in such a plan at an early stage and was rumoured to be a millionairess when she retired. The funny thing is that she never told her husband about it!

A distinction should be made between two different types of ESOPs.

One type comes in the form of options to purchase shares at a fixed price at some future date. The Toronto Stock Exchange study found that 54% of the companies listed on the Exchange offered participation to their employees in the form of such "option plans".

The other type is a "share plan" which allow employees to voluntarily purchase shares. Financial assistance is frequently offered by the company to facilitate the purchase and in some cases the shares may even be bought outright on behalf of the employee.

Share plans are less common. Thus, the Toronto Stock Exchange study found that only 23% of their listed companies had such plans.

Share plans come in two varieties. Either the employee owns the shares directly or the shares are put into a trust and held on his account.

It has been suggested by two authorities on the subject, that direct ownership is more effective than holding shares in a trust.

The best way to review the subject of ESOPs is to consider the advantages and disadvantages.

Advantages of an ESOP from the Viewpoint of the Business

1) The most obvious is that it generates cash that can be invested in the company.

2) It enables the company to pay part of its employees wages in the form of shares and charge this as an operating expense for tax purposes.

3) It may enable the company to attract high calibre or highly skilled employees that it might otherwise be unable to afford. In this sense it allows a small business to compete with larger employers who already have benefit packages in place.

4) Ownership helps stimulate employee loyalty and reduce turnover.

5) Ownership definitely increases productivity according to separate studies conducted for the New York and Toronto Stock Exchanges.

6) Ownership significantly reduces employee absenteeism.

7) Employee ownership can result in serious suggestions to improving company operations and efficiency.

8) Pride of ownership reduces wastage in supplies and material. It also results in greater care taken with company equipment.

9) Employee ownership significantly reduces the chances of strike action and work stoppages.

10) Ownership helps to improve the quality of a company's products since employees take greater care in the production process.

Disadvantages of an ESOP from the Viewpoint of the Company

1) If a lot of employees leave at the one time, there may be a significant drain on cash resources if the company has to re-purchase the shares (which is normally the case with agreements where shares are not listed on a stock exchange).

2) If the company is doing poorly, employee morale may be badly affected. Such causes may be beyond the control of the employees such as, declining markets, poor economy etc.

3) There are legal and accounting costs associated with implementing such plans. In the case of very small companies these costs can be very high relative to the amount of money raised.

4) There is a possible loss of voting control by management and a perceived loss of control over a company's destiny. What happens if there is dissent amongst shareholder-employees on how the company should be run?

5) Unions tend not to take kindly to employee shares ownership schemes and could be hostile to such arrangements.

6) If only some of the employees are offered the opportunity to participate, then discontent may arise amongst those who have been excluded.

7)   The company may become too bottom line oriented. Everything may be focused towards maximizing profits at the expense of putting money into areas that will allow the company to expand. Such might be the case with expenditures on research and development for new products.

8)   Management becomes more accountable to workers for their actions and must be prepared to improve their communications with them.

From the employee's point of view there is the psychological advantage of owning part of the company. However, there are disadvantages.

Disadvantages of ESOPs from the Employee's Point of View

1)   The employee has to pay tax on any portion of the shares that was paid for by the company.

2)   For companies whose shares are not listed on a stock exchange, there is likely to be no market for the shares other than for the company to re-purchase them.

3)   If the company fails (as quite a number of small businesses do), the employee may end up with nothing to show for the investment.

4)   The employee may be psychologically blackmailed into reducing any demands for increased wages or improved working conditions because of the entailed cost to the company.

5)   The Toronto Stock Exchange study found that many ESOP participants felt that they exercised very little control over the day-to-day running of the

company or in the decision making process. Their participation simply relegated them to the role of a minority shareholder.

Points to consider when establishing an ESOP

When establishing an ESOP, consideration must be given to the type of stock to be issued and a mechanism for determining a fair value of the shares.

Procedures also have to be established for the sale of shares to the employees. Employee representation on the board of directors may also have to be addressed.

In the case of unlisted companies, arrangements must be made for their re-purchase in the event of an employee leaving, retiring or dying.

Improved employee performance

The Toronto Stock Exchange study found a considerably improved financial performance on the part of companies with ESOPs compared to those without them.

Profit margins, growth and return on equity were all higher. Whilst the study did not consider unlisted companies, it is reasonable to assume that such an improved financial performance may also apply to them as well.

ESOPs can provide many smaller businesses with badly needed injections of equity capital. This is an area where ESOPs could perform a useful role, especially for the start-up company.

81

Sub-contracting

Subcontracting can prove to be an effective method of keeping wage costs under control in certain instances. This is particularly the case when the volume of work is insufficient to justify full-time employment of a skilled person; or where expensive equipment is required in the preparation of an item.

Subcontracting can be used with everything, from bookkeeping to metal cutting; from silk screening to injection moulding. In fact, subcontracting is very common in small business.

The unit costs of subcontracting may be higher than performing the task internally; but the overall savings of not having to have a skilled person permanently on the payroll could be greater; assuming that the job is intermittent in nature.

In many instances, there may actually be savings in subcontracting. The subcontractor may have sophisticated equipment that will perform the task much faster.

An example might be a firm selling Masonite that will cut to size for their customers. They may operate saws that will cut a large number of sheets at one time which could make the job much cheaper than doing it in-house on a sheet-by-sheet basis.

Because a subcontractor is being paid premium rates, productivity is often (but not always) higher. An added bonus may be better quality of work and accuracy.

The converse of the above argument is - do you have any idle equipment time that could be used to subcontract to others? If so, could this generate added revenue?

Labour & Sub-trades in the Construction Industry

Reliance on, and availability of, sub-trades will have to be addressed. Labour relations and unions relating to those sub-trades will require discussion.

Insurance, workmen's compensation and in particular the costs of third party liability insurance will need to be addressed.

8

MARKETING AND ADVERTISING

In a previous chapter, we looked at how to do market research and how to go about developing a marketing plan. In this chapter, we will look at some of the basic concepts involved in marketing and advertising from a small business perspective.

The Five Basic Elements of Marketing

Whether you are a manufacturer of widgets, an insurance agent or a professional house painter, there are five basic elements in marketing:

1)   You have to use advertising and promotion to make people aware of your product or service;

2)   You have to close the sale and have some kind of order capture system;

3)   You perform order fulfilment in which the product or service is delivered to the customer;

4)   You have to get paid for providing the product or service; and,

5)   You use after-sales service (where applicable) to make sure that the customer is happy and will do repeat business with you.

The Marketing of Products

In the case of a physical product, marketing involves more than just "advertising" - it involves getting that product from the place where it is manufactured and into the hands of the consumer.

As many new, start-up business owners have discovered after they have developed their new and super proverbial "mouse trap", that the world will not beat a path to their door. They have to let the world know about their wonderful new invention and the benefits that it offers mankind. There are many "traditional" ways to do this: telling friends, networking at social or business gatherings, through press releases, advertising in newspapers, magazines, on radio, television, direct mailings, flyers, broadcast faxes, participating in talk shows, writing articles, yellow page advertising, directory listings and advertising, exhibiting at trade shows, sales visits to customers, retailers, potential distributors or wholesalers, etc., etc.

Secondly, there has to be some kind of order capture system. This can vary from a purchase order to a cash register receipt. It creates the paper or electronic trail that allows inventories to be updated, sales taxes to be recorded, invoices to be issued etc. In other words, some system has to be in place to permit the customer to say "yes, I want it" and for the manufacturer or supplier to use this information in what is traditionally known as the "back end".

Thirdly, the manufacturer has to physically get the product into the hands of the customer. In the case of most retail stores, the customer (if he or she is lucky enough to find a car park within 10 light years) enters the store, picks up the product from the shelf and takes it to the line-up at the cash desk. In the case of catalogue companies, direct mail and other direct marketers, the goods are delivered to the customer by courier, delivery van or post office.

In Cyberspace, two scenarios are possible:

a)   The goods can be delivered electronically. This could be the case for software, electronic newspapers, magazines, music, videos, photographs, TV programs, radio shows etc.

b)   The goods cannot be delivered electronically. This would be the case for a new hot-tub, a digital camera, a new computer etc. Obviously, in these instances, there is no difference between the "non-cyberspace world" and "the cyberspace world" and the goods have to be delivered by traditional means.

Fourthly, the manufacturer has to be paid for the products sold. Many marketing "purists" might contend that this is not part of marketing, but if the manufacturer is not paid for the goods, they won't be around for long. Indeed, getting paid has been a factor, that up until now, has put a constraint on the marketing of goods over the Internet. This is changing and will be the subject of more detailed discussion later in the text.

Lastly, the wise marketer will provide after-sales service on the product (wherever this is applicable), to make sure that the customer is happy and will place a repeat order when it comes time to buy again.

Some Factors to Consider When Marketing Products

You may want to reflect on the following factors when you are planning your approach to marketing your products.

Market Niche

Consider the uniqueness of your product and the needs it will satisfy. Alternatively, if your product is not unique, think about the area of the market you will cover and how you expect to establish yourself in the face of competition.

Market Research

Review and summarize any market research that has been done on your product either by yourselves or by other people. Think about any future research that will be required to improve the marketing of existing products or to develop the market for new ones.

Customer Profile

Write out a profile of your typical customer. What segment of the population or what type of companies would buy what you have to offer? This is particularly important when trying to expand your market and find other companies or individuals who match these profiles so that you can make them aware of your products by targeting your advertising and sales efforts.

Total Market Size

Make a calculation of the total number of customers that could use what you are selling. Don't forget your potential export markets. Whilst statistics on foreign markets are sometimes hard to obtain, you can always generalize. Thus, the US market is often considered to be about ten times the size of the Canadian market.

Market Growth

You should find out whether you are in an industry that is growing or dying. Is the total market growing in size or declining? If so - by how much?

Market Penetration

It is useful to prepare an estimate of the percentage of the total market which you would hope to penetrate during the next four or five years. This will give you some idea of where you want to be with respect to your industry group.

Proposed Distribution or Selling Method

Think about how you are going to sell your product e.g., through retail stores; through wholesalers; through jobbers; by direct sales force or by means of sales agents, etc.

Sales Support & Lead Generation

Depending on your product or service, you may wish to attend trade shows in order to promote your product and to generate sales leads for your salespeople or sales agents. You may wish to place advertisements in newspapers or trade journals or you may wish to introduce your product through direct mail to potential customers.

Advertising is necessary to generate product awareness. It can also be used to assist in lead generation.

An example might be an injection moulding machine. This is hardly an item that would be picked up in a retail store but a potential customer might place an enquiry as a result of seeing an advertisement in a trade magazine; as a result of direct mail advertising or as a consequence of visiting a trade show.

All these and other means can be used to generate sales leads for a salesman to make an appointment. Consideration should be given to both advertising and methods of lead generation when preparing your marketing strategy.

Packaging and merchandising

Packaging is vitally important, especially for many lower ticket items. It is the package that often sells the product.

Laundry washing powders may have very similar or identical characteristics so far as the consumer is concerned, however, it is often the packaging that assists the consumer in making a final choice. Mind you, this is frequently done in conjunction with price.

If you are developing a product where the packaging is important, try to make up some dummy cartons or packages. Get some art students to do some rough layouts for you and paste them onto the boxes.

If you have the time and the money, try different types of packaging and vary the colours and then do some tests to see which one people like the most. Conduct tests and ask the opinion of your friends and employees which designs they like best. Document the results and use them in your marketing plan.

If the product lends itself to being sold in a merchandiser or display of some type, then consideration should be given to sketching out a merchandising stand and making up a sample if possible.

The Marketing of Services

What was said above about letting people know about your product is also applicable to services. Whether it be those offered by a stockbroker, a banker, an accountant, a professional house painter, a dentist, an insurance agent etc. They all have to let the consumer know of their existence and what they offer or perish!

In most cases, the order capture process is similar to that for products. In the case of lawyers and some consultants, money is required up front as a retainer. Dentists and others, "extract" it from you (or your insurance company) after they have done their painful work.

Services can be divided into those that can be delivered electronically and those that can't.

Some services have to be delivered at your place of residence or work e.g., the house painter, the bookkeeper, the plumber. Others require that you go to their premises e.g., the dentist, the lawyer, the restaurant, except for home delivered pizzas, etc.

The electronic delivery of services is relatively new. We can now gamble in cyberspace. When enough bandwidth becomes available, we will be able to view movies on a pay-per-view basis or listen to music on a "pay-per-listen" basis.

We can also bank electronically without visiting the banking establishment. You will notice that I have avoided using the word "cyberspace" in this context since electronic banking does not necessarily have to be conducted over the Internet although the trend is in that direction.

In the case of a stockbroker we have always been able to conduct trades over the phone with our broker, without visiting the establishment, however, electronic trading using the Internet has taken off in recent years.

So essentially, delivery of services is not too dissimilar to the delivery of goods.

The issues relating to payment and after-sales service are also similar to those for products.

Some Factors to Consider When Marketing Services

If you are planning a service company, you should consider the size of the market that is to be served together with the potential for expansion.

If it is possible to conduct some market research and include the results of these studies, so much the better.

Again, it is important to define the profile of typical customers - especially their financial status and how much your service depends on their disposable income if your customers are individuals rather than corporations.

You should try to estimate your share of the market. The word "penetration" is not appropriate here. In order to make these calculations you will have to know the approximate size of the whole market and express your share as a percentage.

In the case of start-ups, compare the number of beds or the number of seats that you will be offering with the total number for the town. You could further relate these figures to the total population of the town and to the number of visitors. (Your Chamber of Commerce or your government tourist department should be able to help you with these numbers).

Similarly, if you are starting a restaurant, you should compare the number of seats that will be offered with the total number of seats available in restaurants throughout the area.

Image

A professional image counts a great deal, especially in the service and retail industries. Give consideration to uniforms, caps, logos, painted vans and anything that will help to enhance your status as a provider of that service.

If you ever have to seek outside financing, from a bank or an investor, they are more likely to be impressed if you have given some though to this matter.

What could be worse than having your staff drive up to a customer's residence in a rusty old van and are dressed in tattered jeans?

Advertising and Sales Lead Generation for a Service Business

Once more, you should consider the most appropriate methods of advertising and sales lead development. You should also think about any warranties that may be applicable to the service which you offer.

You should think about whether your service offers the possibility of repeat business and you might want to consider a customer loyalty program to try and retain your customers. Give them a small gift or a discount, after they have accumulated a number of sales points.

Marketing and Advertising for Retailers

If you are going to open a shop, you should consider the exclusivity of any products that you are offering and your pricing policies. The retail business is highly competitive; what with discount stores and sales made over the Internet.

In the area of town in which I live, I find it very depressing that every year there is a tremendous turnover of retail stores and restaurants. The ones that seem to survive are those that offer some unique or specialized service or are open as convenience stores for very long hours.

The retail business is a tough business and having previously run a display company which made fixturing for retail stores, I can tell you from first-hand experience that many retailers are hanging in there by their finger nails.

Do the Number Crunching!

It is useful to calculate what your gross margins will be, according to product categories. Thus, if you own a greengrocers store, you might find that the gross profits on cut flowers are far greater than on oranges or lettuce. On the other hand, flowers may not last very long and have a high wastage factor.

You should consider your total market size within your area; a profile of your typical customer groups and your market share.

If you are thinking about purchasing an existing retail operation, conduct a "Bottom Up" analysis in which you count the average number of passersby and compare these with the number of people who actually enter the store.

You can take this a stage further and compare the number of people who actually made a purchase as a percentage of those who enter the store. You might also want to include an estimate of impulse sales as opposed to planned purchases by customers. Most drug store operators will tell you that about half of their sales were unplanned (or impulse) when the shopper went into the store to purchase something else.

This is the same reason that most convenience stores place the fridge with their milk at the rear of the store so that you have to walk past all the food displays, candies, snacks and other goodies before you can select the item you went in for.

In the case of a start-up, you could perform this analysis by observing someone else's store selling the same products in the town by counting the number of people who enter their store compared with those who walk by. You could then compare these figures with the number of people who walk by your proposed location. It could give you a rough estimate of your potential store traffic.

Advertising for Retailers

Consider the forms of external advertising that you propose to use - radio, newspaper, TV, flyers or direct mail? Which is likely to be the most effective and why? How much will this advertising cost on a per customer basis? How much will it cost per additional customer obtained as a result of running the ad?

What forms of internal advertising do you propose? Discuss your proposed outside signage, window signs and in-store signage. How effective will your displays be - your window dressing or point of sale stands within the store?

Warranties & Returned Goods

This applies to retailers but it also relates to manufacturers. Will you offer any warranties? What will be your policy about returned goods? What percentage of your sales do you expect to be returned?

Competition & Customer Loyalty

Whether you are a manufacturer, service company or retailer, you want to try to develop customer loyalty. What percentage of your customers will come back?

What is your competition? Sit in a restaurant or car park and do a bottom-up analysis on them. How many customers walk into the location. Make an estimate of how much they spend. Compare this to the approximate cost of rent for that location. Take into account the cost of employee wages, business taxes and the probable profit margins for the products that are being sold. You'll start to get an idea of how profitable the business is.

Another factor to consider, if you will be selling expensive items, is whether you will offer credit or financing plans.

Promotion

If your product or service lends itself to promotions through incentives offered to those using it, this should be taken into consideration in preparing the marketing strategy. Visit some of the premium and marketing trade shows. You may come away with hundreds of ideas.

9

PRICING YOUR PRODUCT OR SERVICE

Use Your Test Marketing to Set Prices

The test marketing can also be used to test different prices in different markets. It does not always follow that the lowest price is the one that achieves the highest sales volume.

Sometimes, consumers will pay a higher price in the belief that the value is greater. A classic in this regard was when the cold medicine "Contact C" was test marketed, volume of sales of the product bearing a price of $1.69 was three times higher than that of the same product bearing a price of $0.99.

This example should caution the entrepreneur to be careful in avoiding the trap of cutting prices in order to increase volume. Many make the mistake of attempting to increase sales by discounting. Remember, that a big profit margin on a low sales volume can often be better that a slim profit margin on a high sales volume!

Marketing "quality" often means selling at higher prices than the competition.

Pricing is a function of demand for a product relative to its available supply. The introduction of the Cabbage Patch Doll a few years ago provided a classic illustration of high price associated with scarce supply which lasted during that introductory period.

Pricing is also a function of "elasticity" of the product - how necessary is it? Basic foodstuffs and shelter are relatively "inelastic" in-so-far as people have to have them. Luxuries such as VCRs or Cabbage Patch Dolls are very elastic because people can exist quite well without them.

Pricing Strategies

An important element of self- financing your business from internally generated profits is product pricing. If the pricing strategy isn't right, then the business may simply not be able to grow.

Your pricing strategy should be aimed at achieving the maximum profits for the company. It should not be aimed at achieving maximum sales!

It may be better to sell a small quantity of a product on which there is a high profit, than a large quantity of a product on which there is only a very small profit. The latter might be justified where a loss lead item is used to attract customers to do business with the firm (and hopefully purchase other items!).

There are many strategies, depending on what the business wants to accomplish.

Inventory clearouts can be achieved with low pricing. Discounters rely on low prices to take business away from competitors. They have to make up for decreased margins through increased volumes or more efficient operations.

Companies selling unique or prestigious items, or goods that are in short supply, may be able to command higher prices than would otherwise be the case. Some may be able to justify such prices by stressing the quality of their goods.

Another strategy might be to force competition out of the business through low prices or carve out a larger market share or in order to be regarded as an industry leader. Such a strategy may be fine on its own - but the competition seldom "plays dead".

The main objective, in both the long or short run, is to maximize profits through a pricing strategy. Remember, that increased volume often increases variable costs! More staff may be required; more equipment etc.

A proper pricing strategy has to be worked out by the small business owner on an individual basis. The process can be greatly assisted by people with experience of the market and by good market research.

9

FINANCIAL PROJECTIONS

Fixed and Variable Costs

The distinction should be made between your fixed and variable costs. The following discussion relates to a manufacturing business.

Variable costs are those which vary in accordance with your production. They include all the expenses that are directly related to your production, such as the wages of the production workers, materials used in the production, delivery and freight costs, etc.

Fixed costs, on the other hand, are those which you would incur even if your production operations were closed down. Thus, you would still have to pay rent, bank charges, insurance, interest on any loans, together with the wages of employees that are not directly involved in the production process.

Gross Profit Margin

Your gross profit margin on the product that you're producing, is the difference between the direct costs incurred in producing it and the price for which it is sold. Taking our widget example, let us say that each widget sells for $10, and requires materials costing three dollars and incurs a labour cost of four dollars to produce it, then the gross profit margin is three dollars.

Break-Even Point

Continuing with the above example, the fact that you are making a gross profit of three dollars per widget does not necessarily mean that the business is now profitable, because you have to take into account your fixed costs. To illustrate this, let us say that you produce 3 widgets per hour, equivalent to 1,200 widgets per week (based on a 40 hour week). This would produce a gross profit of $3,600 per week.

It is quite possible that your fixed costs may be greater than $3,600 per week, in which case the business is generating a loss. This would be quite possible if your paying $1,000 per week in rent; if you have a bookkeeper, receptionist, order desk clerk, sales representative each earning an average of $600 per week and you have office expenses, telephone bills, postage, insurance, utilities, automobile expenses, advertising costs, etc., amounting to $1,000 per week. If you add those expenses, you will arrive at a total off $4,400, which means that the business is losing $800 per week.

On the other hand, if the bookkeeper also acts as receptionist and order desk clerk, you will have eliminated two people from a payroll, thereby saving $1200 per week. In such a case, the business would be making a profit before taxes of $400 per week.

If you follow this simplistic example and assume that your fixed costs amount to $3,600 per week, which is the same as your gross profit, then the you have reached your breakeven point. In other words, you are not making any profit, but on the other hand you are not losing anything either.

Most new businesses lose money during their initial start-up, and it can take them several months (or even years) to reach their breakeven point. This serves to illustrate that the new business owner must have sufficient cash reserves to see them through the start-up period.

Preparing Your Projections

I would strongly recommend that you learn how to use a spreadsheet before attempting to prepare any projections, because it makes life so much easier when you do the number crunching and "what ifs" by changing some of your assumptions.

Take a course or read some books on bookkeeping or accounting. This would also be very helpful. As a consultant, I have been amazed at the number of new business owners who can't read a financial statement--or who do not have a grasp on basic accounting principles. Do yourself a favour if you do not have these skills--try to acquire them or at least try to grasp the general principles involved. At least you will be able to have an intelligent discussion with your accountant when the time comes.

Sales Projections

Prepare your sales projections for the next five years and think about what percentage of the market you expect to penetrate each year. Show your sales in units of product and total dollar value.

Capital Budget

Compile a list of equipment, vehicles or other assets which you will need to purchase in order to carry on the business. The list should also include the estimated cost of each item and should be totalled at the bottom of the page.

Financial Projections

Prepare your financial projections and pay attention to when you expect to break even. I would strongly recommend that you prepare cash flow projections on a monthly basis for the next two years (see the discussion of cash flow in a previous chapter). I would then suggest preparing the same cash flow projections, but on a quarterly basis for the next three years.

If you have the bookkeeping or accounting know-how to take this a stage further, then I would also recommend the preparation of profit and loss pro-formas on a monthly basis for the next two years and quarterly for a further three years, together with pro-forma balance sheets.

Planogramming - A Powerful Tool for Retailers

If you are already operating a retail business and you have the figures from cash register departments, you may wish to calculate your sales per square foot by department (referred to as planogramming). This analysis can be quite revealing, particularly if it is combined with gross margins to come up with a profit picture on a square foot basis by department or section in your store.

You can lay this out graphically by colouring in a floor plan; using different colours for different ranges of gross profits. It will tell you pretty quickly what areas of the store are making money and what areas are not. It will tell you what mechandise is making money from you and the lines that you might consider dropping or repositioning.

Other Factors Retailers Should Consider

You should think about the quantity of inventory that you have to maintain and the lead times for replacement. There is little point in displaying 100 widgets on the shelf, if you only sell two per week. You might be better off with only four on the shelf and keep re-ordering each week on a just-in-time basis, The downfall of this is that you may be faced with a minimum order quantity or the delivery costs may not justify re-ordering at such frequent intervals.

Don't forget that money is tied up in maintaining inventory. This is a critical factor at the start-up stage when funds may be limited and you may not be sure of what will sell and what will not. So, maintaining inventory on a just-in-time basis is a great concept, even though it may be difficult to enact in practice.

You should also try to find out how many times you turned your merchandise over during the year. Did you sell out the display rack one time, three times or ten times? This can usually only be done on a department basis in conjunction with figures from the cash register. Obviously, you want to sell items with a high turnover.

10

DO YOU HAVE ENOUGH MONEY?

Can You Start The Business With Your Own Money?

In the case of start-up and early stage financing, personal resources are very important. A study by the Creative Research Group found that two-thirds to three-quarters of the average investment for start-ups in Ontario of $25,000 was put up by the entrepreneur himself or herself. These figures clearly demonstrate a lack of readily available outside financing for companies at the start-up stage.

In the case of established small and medium-sized growth companies, a more recent study by Statistics Canada (*Strategies for Success - A Profile of Growing Small and Medium-sized Enterprises (GSMEs) In Canada*) revealed that 29.9% of financing for such companies came from internally generated funds or retained earnings.

This underscores the fact that small business owners have a hard time in obtaining start-up financing from outside sources. This is especially so if the owner lacks any significant collateral (such as home or other assets) that can be posted as collateral for a bank loan.

The Personal Financial Statement

The easiest way of coming to a decision as to whether to go it alone or not, is to prepare a personal financial statement in order to determine your true financial position. To achieve this, you will need to calculate your personal assets (what you own) and your personal liabilities (what you owe).

<u>Assets</u>

```
Cash in bank or savings...........$_____
Stocks or bonds at market value...$_____
Real estate at market value.......$_____
Automobile at market value........$_____
Other assets at market value......$_____

TOTAL ASSETS......................$_____
```

<u>Liabilities</u>

```
Bank loans........................$_____
Mortgage..........................$_____
Credit card balances..............$_____
Installment purchases.............$_____
Personal taxes that will be due
or are owning.....................$_____
Any other financial commitments...$_____

TOTAL LIABILITIES.................$_____
```

In arriving at your net worth, you will want to subtract what you owe (your liabilities) from what you own (your assets).

You can now compare this final figure with the financial requirements of the business. At that point, it would be useful to go back to your cash flow statements which were discussed earlier and see what is the minimum cash requirement to keep the business in the black.

When you start your own business, it becomes a personal judgement call as to whether or not you will go ahead using your own funds and if so, what portion of them you will commit to the business. If you use other people's funds, you will likely have to post a large portion of your assets as security for the loan.

Financing While Working Elsewhere

There has been many a wise person who has started a business on the side, whilst working for somebody else. Such an arrangement can provide a temporary cash flow (over and above living expenses) to float the new business.

The big disadvantage of such an arrangement is the lack of time which it provides to start the business properly. A new operation requires hours and hours of dedicated work and total commitment. This may be very difficult to make, if one has to spend eight hours working for someone else to bring in the bacon.

Credit Cards

It may sound facetious, but people have actually financed their start-ups with cash advances made on their credit cards!

The advantages are that no collateral is required and no approval necessary for what the funds are to be used for.

The disadvantages are that interest rates are usually very high and the money has to be paid back, even though this may be in stages, just as with any other loan. Enough said!

Can the Business Finance Itself?

A study in Venture Magazine some years ago indicated that some 9% of start-ups finance themselves from internally generated cash. The Venture study showed that this form of financing provided more than twice the amount of capital obtained from venture capital sources (4%) and almost twice that from private placements (5%).

An Ontario study found that only about half of all new business owners required additional capital after they had started. The implicit assumption is, that the other half were generating sufficient funds internally to sustain themselves and to expand. ["Newly-Formed Small Businesses in Ontario 1982-1984", Ontario Ministry of Industry, Trade and Technology.]

Figures from Statistics Canada indicate that, for companies with annual revenues of under $5 million, 36.5% of their capital requirements come from internally generated funds. ["Small Business in Canada" 1991, Industry, Science and Technology, Canada]

Indeed, if you can make enough widgets in your basement (using your own seed money to build them) and sell them from the trunk of your car, you may be able to make a handsome profit!

This money made from such sales could in turn be used to employ somebody to work in your basement with you while you go out on the road selling. This will allow you to produce more, since one person is now fully occupied in manufacturing. The additional money which you make may allow you to hire a second person for production... then a sales representative.

The next step might be to find a small manufacturing space that is not too expensive. This will allow you to employ three more people in production and put a second sales rep on the road. So on it goes!

Will the Cash Flow Be Adequate?

If you refer back to the discussion of cash flow in an earlier chapter and our proverbial bath tub, the question that has to be asked here is whether there is enough water flowing into the bath tub from the profit tap to exceed the amount flowing out through the drain.

Maybe it is best to qualify what I mean. Most businesses require some initial capital, for example, our window washing service company will probably need squeegees, detergent, pails, a ladder and if he is high minded, a rope, a pulley, a mobile scaffold (and lots of courage).

113

The question is, after that initial expenditure, can the business run itself without additional capital being added?

"After the initial expenditure?" you say. "And if I spend a million dollars initially? The trouble is - I don't have the dough!" Herein, lies the trap in our generalization. By self-financing, we are making the assumption that the initial seed capital is relatively modest.

Let's go back to the window washing example. Assume that for the first job, the window washer borrows a bucket and a ladder. He goes to his local hardware store and purchases some detergent and a squeegee. He's in business!

When he collects enough money he buys his own ladder and bucket. The assumption made in this chapter is that the initial requirements are relatively modest and can be financed internally, out of pocket, without the necessity of approaching outside sources.

Some Preliminary Considerations

Before you can determine whether the business will finance itself, you have to look at your own available resources.

Does the business owner have the resources in the form of manpower and equipment etc., to go it alone and achieve its objectives? If it has, then by all means sail your own ship because this is the cheapest form of capital you can possibly obtain.

What is Bootstrap Financing?

Bootstrap financing is the method of generating capital from the internal operations of a company. In essence, the financing is provided by the company itself without the involvement of any outsiders. There are no bank loans, no participation by venture capitalists and probably the only initial injection of cash was from the owner's savings. Thereafter, the show runs itself.

Bootstrap financing has the advantage that entrepreneurs can run their own show without having to rely on financial partners. They can wake up in the morning and not have to worry about whether the bank is going to call their loans. It provides freedom from outside interference that may have attracted them to do "their own thing" in the first place.

Financing by bootstrapping can be used to develop a company to a stage that it becomes attractive for outside financing.

Venture capitalists may show a reluctance to invest in a start-up or early stage company and if they do, they are likely to want a large portion of the ownership. The same venture capitalists, however, may be quite willing to invest at a later stage when the company has shown that it is profitable. At this point the amount of ownership that the entrepreneur has to give up is likely to be much less.

Bootstrap financing has the disadvantage that the business may not be able to grow as fast as it might have with the assistance of outside financial help. It can only grow as fast as it can generate enough money for expansion. Such financing can be a severe limiting factor on the speed of a company's growth.

Bootstrap financing requires a substantial amount of control over business operations. For example, it requires vigilance to ensure that the monies owing it from customers (called "receivables") are coming in promptly to finance growth.

If the controls are not in place, then things can become so fouled-up that the financial health of the company may be jeopardized and any potential growth stunted. Bootstrap financing requires management in the fast lane to be really successful.

12

SEEKING OUTSIDE INVESTORS

In this chapter we will take a look at some of the places where you can obtain start-up capital for your business.

Love Money

"Love money" is the term used to describe investments made by relatives and friends.

It is a significant source of financing for start-ups. According to an Ontario study, relatives and friends provided 15% of the start-up funding for the incorporated companies studied and 31% for the unincorporated ones [Creative Research Group in their study: *Newly-Formed Businesses in Ontario, 1982-1984*].

A similar study in Venture Magazine suggested that loans from relatives and friends accounted for 11% of the capital for start-ups [*Venture* Magazine, October 1985].

Canada's classic example of an entrepreneur who raised financing from "love money" was the inventor of the game "Trivial Pursuit". It is reported that Derrick

Ramsey, then a copy boy for the Montreal Gazette, invested $1,000 in this scheme only to find his investment grow to $1/2 million! [*Your Money*, September/October 1985]

Friends and relatives could be looked to for direct small cash investments or for loan guarantees. However, if the venture goes off track and ends up in the swamp, you may wake up one morning to find that, not only do you not have a business, but you don't have any friends or relatives left either!

Some anonymous advice from Evan Esar's *20,000 Quips and Quotes* may be appropriate: "Neither a borrower or a lender be: if you're a borrower, you'll have distant relatives; if you're a lender, you'll have close ones."

And some advice on where to find wealthy relatives: "Some relatives are distant, some are close, but the wealthiest are both distant and close." You are on your own on this one!

Venture Capital

It is difficult to arrive at an all-encompassing definition, however, the venture capital has certain characteristics that distinguish it from other sources of capital.

Firstly, the money is normally unsecured. It is provided without collateral or any net to fall into should the deal fall off the high wire. Having said this, however, a venture capitalist will usually attempt to obtain as much security as possible for the risk that he is taking. Such security might be in the form of assignment of assets or whatever guarantees he can obtain.

Secondly, the venture capitalist prefers equity ownership in the business because that is how he makes his money. When the business increases in value, he can sell out at a higher price. Some will provide loans and loan guarantees - but usually in combination with equity.

Thirdly, he does not normally say, "here's your money - get on with it!" He frequently wants to become involved with the venture and tries to use his skills in building (what he hopes) will become a successful business. This involvement isn't in the form of day-to-day management, but rather in the form of advice, assistance and where necessary, "insistence" on improving management practices and strategies. Many venture capitalists can bring a lot of experience to the companies they invest in.

Fourthly, he is usually involved in a deal for anywhere from three to ten years. He has to be a patient fellow, because it takes a long time for his deals to mature and bear fruit. Unlike a player in the stock market, who might be in and out of a deal in a couple of months, the venture capitalist is a medium- to long-term investor.

The history of venture capital dates back to the trading expeditions of the middle ages. Some of these ended up ship-wrecked on windswept coral islands. Others fared a little better and a few yielded their participants magnificent returns on their investments.

One such expedition was the 1577-1580 voyage of Sir Francis Drake, which produced returns of 4,600% on the initial investments of the backers! This was after Queen Elizabeth I of England had skimmed her share off the top! [Herbert Heaton: Economic History of Europe"]

The formal North American venture capital market, as we know it today, began with modest beginnings after World War II.

The amount of money under management has multiplied at a fast rate since that time. Much of the growth in the United States can be attributed to help provided by the Small Business Investment Companies Act, which gave venture capital investors tax advantages together with easy access to government borrowing.

However, the big growth in the market was spurred on by the high rates of return achieved by a number of companies during the earlier days of the high tech boom era.

There is the story of how a Harvard professor, by the name of Doriot, established the American Research and Development Corp., a venture capital company, which over a period of 14 years, saw an initial investment of $70,000 in Apple Computers grow to an estimated $350 million.

Successes such as this, attracted investors to the North American venture capital industry in the same way bees are attracted to honey or, as some might put it a little less kindly, the same way as vultures are attracted to a kill!

The industry preferences of venture capitalists are healy geared towards technologies, which cover the whole spectrum biotechnology, communications, computer related, electronics, energy/environmental technologies, industrial automation and equipment and those that are medical or health related.

The entrepreneur should be alerted to the fact that very few start-up companies actually succeed in raising venture capital. This fact is very sobering and reflects the harsh reality of the venture capital market as a source for start-up funding.

Informal Investors Or "Angels"

The term "Angel", as a financing source, owes its origin to Broadway in the 1930's when it was applied to individual investors who provided financial backing for the plays and musicals of that time.

Its use was furthered during the late 1970's by the work of Professor William Wetzel of the Whittimore School of Business and Economics at the University of New Hampshire. He conducted a study for the United States Small Business Administration on the availability of informal risk capital in the New England States.

The results of the study drew attention to a little recognized, but widely accepted method of start-up and small business financing - namely the tapping of available private sources of money.

The term "Angel" has now been widely accepted by the North American financial and venture capital communities, as describing the individual; informal investor who is prepared to invest risk capital in junior companies. Many of his investments are made in start-up or early stage firms.

Several other terms have also been used to describe angels. The most common is "venture capitalist", however, informal investors are not organized in the same manner and usually the deals they invest in are much smaller.

Another term which has been used in Canada is "Individual Venture Investor" or IVI. The latter has an unfortunate connotation and may conjure up the image of needles. For that reason, the author prefers the cleaner and somewhat more pristine term of "angel".

The Funding Gap

It has become generally recognized that funding requirements in the $50,000 to $1/2 million range; especially for start-up and early stage situations, are very difficult to obtain. In general, these are too large to raise from family or friends and often too small to be of interest to the "traditional" venture capitalist.

This funding gap has been repeatedly recognized in government studies. It was confirmed in the House of Commons Report of the Standing Committee on Industry of October 1994. It was recognized in the Report of the Manitoba Task Force on Capital Markets in July 1994, which divided "the gap" into two discernable areas:

- "Less than fully secured" debt and equity financing of $50,000 to $250,000 for start-ups and first stage expansion; and

- Equity financing in the $250,000 to $1 million range for all financing stages.

It costs the traditional venture capitalist as much time and money to investigate a small deal as it does a larger one. In many cases, it takes longer because of the lack of management skills that frequently characterize small businesses.

By the time the traditional venture capitalist has analyzed the situation; had his lawyers and accountants scrutinize it and has drawn up shareholder agreements, he will have dipped quite deeply into his pocket, especially if he can't immediately recover these costs from the small business owner, who may not have the funds.

Another problem faced by the traditional venturist relates to the administration of the investment. It is generally claimed that the smaller the company; the more problems that arise and the more time that has to be spent correcting them.

A hard fact that has to be digested by the entrepreneur, is that these problems make investments of under $1/2 million unattractive to the traditional venture capitalist. It is a pity, because most small businesses only require funding of under this amount.

The problem of the funding gap is not confined to Canada. It was recognized by the American Small Business Administration, after they had hired Professor Wetzel to look into the problem.

His studies concluded that the best source of funding for small businesses in the early stages was from the informal investor or "angel" community.

The American Experience

Professor Wetzel reported his findings in the Sloan Management Review.

He conducted a survey of 133 informal investors in the New England area. He believed that these represented barely one twentieth of the actual number of informal investors in that community.

Studying the investments made by this research sample led him to the conclusion the angel community probably finances about five times as many ventures as the traditional venture capitalists and the public equity markets combined. He also found that most investments made by angels were in the $20,000 to $50,000 range.

Characteristics of Angels

Angels come in many different shapes and sizes. Professor Wetzel described them as individuals with a net worth of over $250,000 and annual earnings in excess of $50,000. Bear in mind that this study was conducted in the late 1970's so you'll have to allow for inflation!

Basically, angels are wealthy, well-to-do members of the community and include doctors, lawyers, accountants, businessmen and others who are prepared to invest anywhere from a few thousand dollars to a hundred thousand in small businesses.

Angels do not always invest in companies for purely financial reasons. Many have the social goodwill of their community at heart and seek situations that will generate employment or bring other benefits to their community.

Some angels are executives in other businesses whilst others may be retired executives who want to become involved in their investment, rather than taking a passive role. They want to participate on a day-to-day basis or on a week-to-week basis. In many ways, investments for these people take the place of hobbies.

Others are executives who are currently employed and are looking for a change but who don't want to start up their own businesses. They would like to become involved in someone else's and create a senior management position for themselves.

Others want to place themselves in a position (e.g., with stock options) that if the business is successful, they can take over control. This, of course, leads to a potential conflict with the entrepreneur, who may not want somebody looking over his or her shoulder all day and certainly has no desire to give up control of the business in the event that it is successful.

Some angels are former entrepreneurs who have "made it" and rather than sit sunning themselves on the beach, are looking for new investment opportunities. These are the "entrepreneur junkies" who can't sit still unless they get a regular "fix" on a good opportunity. Such people may bring with them an immense amount of experience and knowledge, since many of them have attended the "hard knocks" school on their way to making it big. This is probably the best type of angel an entrepreneur could possibly land.

An angel is really a junior, less formal version of a venture capitalist. The difference between the two is not clear-cut. Like the venture capitalist, the angel is generally a supplier of unsecured credit to junior businesses.

Angels As Risk Takers

In many ways, the angel is more venturesome than the true "venture" capitalist, because he is more likely to venture into start-up situations. That is not to say he is foolish. It is usually his own hard-earned money that he is investing and he will want to make sure that he is not throwing it away in some hair-brained scheme.

As we saw earlier in this book, traditional venture capitalists do not like to invest in start-ups and tend to wait and see some earnings first before investing. In this sense, they are really "expansion" capitalists because they are providing capital for expansion and growth. Angels, on the other hand, like to get into a deal near the beginning.

Angels in Canada

Canada has its own surveyor of angels in the form of Allan Riding, Associate Professor in the School of Business at Carleton University, together with his assistant, Dominique Short. They found that the informal venture capital market in Canada is similar in many respects to that found by Prof. Wetzel for the New England States. Many of the comments which follow are based on the results of their excellent work.

The Significance of Angels

When entrepreneurs and small business owners are asked where they turn to for risk capital, the most frequently cited source is their own pocket book.

The second most common source was angels. Indeed, this confirms that entrepreneurs had already recognized Professor Wetzel's findings in which he suggested that angels provide the largest pool of capital for start-ups and small business.

In fact, in Al Riding's study, angels were cited three times more frequently than traditional venture capitalists as being the place to go in order to obtain financing.

It is interesting that angels even came ahead of relatives as the fountain of money. This can only mean one of two things - either entrepreneurs have poor relatives or they have rich relatives that don't believe in what they are doing!!

An American study suggested that angels made investments of about $5 billion in the United States in 1981. That same year, public underwritings on stock markets amounted to $3.7 billion and venture capitalists invested $2.5 billion. ["Informal Risk Capital - Knowns and Unknowns" prepared for State of the Art in Entrepreneurial Research, RGK Foundation, February 1985]. Whilst these figures are a little outdated, they still indicate where the start-up entrepreneur should focus his or her efforts when seeking capital.

What makes these figures all the more interesting is that the venture capitalist investments seldom invest in small start-ups. Initial Public Offerings on stock markets rarely involve small start-ups. On the other hand, angels tend to invest in start-up and early stage companies. In conducting your search for outside funding, you should recognize that angels supply the vast bulk of outside venture capital requirements for start-up and new developing companies.

For these reasons, the entrepreneur who is serious about seeking equity funding would be well advised to find out all about angels and where to locate them.

Profile of Canadian Angels

Based on interviews conducted by Al Riding and Dominique Short in the Ottawa-Carleton region, angels can be said to have five basic characteristics.

Firstly, they are male and of median age fifty. In this sense, they are not yuppies, but people who have likely acquired a little grey hair or lost it altogether.

Secondly, they are well educated. They tend to have university or college degrees in law, business or engineering.

127

Thirdly, they hold senior managerial or administrative positions. Also included are lawyers, management consultants and other entrepreneurs who have already "made it" or are well on their way to doing so.

Fourthly, they make lots of money. They have an average annual income of $150,000 and two-thirds of them reported incomes in excess of $100,000. (Since this study was done a few years ago, these figures would now be a bit higher due to inflation.)

Fifthly, they have a personal net worth of $1 million. Of course, due to the rapid escalation of real estate prices in certain cities such as Toronto and Vancouver in the late '80s, and the stockmarket boom of the past 17 years, there are more potential angels at that time than ever before.

How Many Angels Are There in Canada?

There are lots of people in Canada who drive Mercedes, but are they actually angels?

Again, Al Riding and Dominique Short conducted a study in the Ottawa-Carleton region. Essentially, this regarded investors in the same manner as biologists wishing to count the population of squirrels in a forest. They tag some of them! This avoids the necessity of a census!

They found that investors gather together in clusters and that the individuals making up these clusters generally had fairly high profiles within the community.

They then compared these active investors (actual angels) with the number of people who fitted the classification but who were not actually investors in small businesses (potential angels).

According to statistics, there were 1,500 - 1,750 people in the region who filed 1986 income tax returns indicating incomes in excess of $100,000. This represented approximately 1/100 of the population of the region.

It was found that only one in twenty (1/20) of these high income earners was actually an angel. It is therefore possible to conclude that only one person in every two thousand (1/20th of 1/100) of the population is a practising angel.

Of course it is possible to extrapolate these figures further. If you have one in every two thousand in Ottawa-Carleton - how many are there in Canada as a whole? If you take the population at 25 million and divide by 2,000, you arrive at a figure of 12,500 angels.

There are some dangers in making such an extrapolation, as Al Riding has warned the author.

Firstly, the Ottawa-Carleton region boasts some of the highest income earners in Canada (thanks to the location there of the Canadian Federal Government).

Secondly, there is a disproportionately large element of high technology associated with Kanata which has been called the "Silicon Valley of the North". This, of course, presents high tech investment opportunities which might not be present in other areas of the country.

So, even if you shave the figure down, it means that there might be about 10,000 active angels in Canada as a whole. That's certainly a lot more than the 70 or 80 venture capital companies!

Using the seat-of-the pants formula that the United States market is ten times the size of the Canadian market, you would expect there to be about 100,000 angels in the US.

Corporate Angels

In addition to individuals, there are companies in the community who have accumulated a positive cash position and are looking for diversification. The author has termed these as: "corporate angels".

Many tend to concentrate on investments that will complement their existing activities. For example, a company in the engraving business might expand into the trophy business (which uses engraving extensively).

Another example might be a company which is marketing a product to a certain group and would be willing to entertain another non-competing product which relates to the same market.

Like the traditional venture capitalist, the corporate angel is generally a supplier of unsecured capital, however, his main activity is running his own business, rather than supplying funds for growing companies. This distinguishes the corporate angel from some large corporations which, either supply funds to outside venture capital companies, or form their own venture capital subsidiaries.

Distributors As Angels

Corporate angels could be potential distributors for your product. They are likely to want some exclusivity on distribution rights.

Such arrangements could be very beneficial to a young firm in providing it with an immediate market outlet for its products. In many instances this could prove more valuable than the injection of cash.

The best place to look for potential dealers or distributors is amongst companies that are already selling non-competitive products to the same market. Thus, if you have come out with a new game of tiddlywinks, your best bet would be to approach toy companies who attend all the toy trade shows and already have sales representatives calling on all the major toy stores and department stores throughout the country.

Suppliers As Angels

Corporate angels might be potential suppliers of components for your product. In this case, your company would represent another marketing outlet for them, in addition to providing them with an investment opportunity.

Such angels may be cautious or reluctant to become involved, if your company end ups in competition to their existing customers with whom they have built up a good relationship over many years. So, your best chances are when you have a new application for something which they produce.

Another possibility is an extension of credit. If you can collect your receivables quickly while paying your suppliers on the extended credit terms they offer you, then you will have created a source of short term financing.

Customers

Corporate angels could be potential users or customers for your product or service.

The big advantage with this type of angel is that they already appreciate the merits of your product and its market. Because they are in a position to understand and grasp the potential of what you have developed, they may be more willing to participate as investors than outsiders who are not so familiar with the market.

Even if your customers are unwilling to put any money on the table, they may be prepared to place a purchase order with you for delivery at a date sometime into the future (say, three or six months). A whole bunch of such purchase orders can do wonders in front of cynical investors, who may have doubts about the viability of your product and the market.

Armed with such orders, you may also find the task of borrowing money much easier.

A customer may be prepared to provide financing without actually becoming a shareholder, however, the practice is not common. He may be willing to pay the small business to develop certain material or equipment that is not readily available elsewhere. He might finance the purchase of materials used in a production run.

Quite frequently, customers will assist in the development of parts that can be used in their own equipment (commonly referred to as OEM or Other Equipment Manufacturers parts). They may offer assistance in the design and testing of parts; even if they don't bring bags of money to the table.

13

BORROWING MONEY FOR YOUR BUSINESS

Debt As Opposed to Equity

This chapter deals with debt financing or the borrowing of money to finance a business or start-up.

Debt financing does not require the giving up of any of the ownership in the business and for that reason, many entrepreneurs prefer it as a form of financing.

Debt financing is generally easier to obtain than equity financing. The six major Canadian Chartered Banks operate about 8,000 branches across the country. In the United States, there are more regional banks, in addition to some with a national network.

Venture capitalists, on the other hand, tend to be centred in a few major cities. Informal investors, called "angels" certainly do not advertise because they prefer their privacy, rather than being inundated with hopeful business plans and proposals.

Debt financing is not a panacea. It has costs attached to it, aside from the obvious interest payments. Collateral requirements can be quite onerous which can ultimately make lending a very, very expensive proposition.

135

The Banking Function

Banks are in business to make money. They do so simply by using other people's money, which they can obtain at a lower rate of interest, and lending it to other people at a higher rate of interest.

In other words, they use money from your chequing accounts (upon which you pay monthly service and statement charges, as you well know!) and low paying savings accounts to invest in much higher yielding government bonds, treasury bills, commercial paper, mortgages, customer loans or anything else with a higher yield. The difference provides them with their bread and butter or in many cases their champagne and caviar!

The sums deposited with banks provide the banks with their "play money", since for every dollar they have on deposit or in reserve they can in turn loan out so many dollars. Thus, if a bank operates with a 10% reserve; for every dollar in reserve, it can loan ten dollars out. If it operates with a 5% reserve, it can loan out $20 and so on.

These comments are obviously an oversimplification of a sophisticated money machine that has been developed over the years. However, an anonymous statement in Evan Esar's *20,000 Quips and Quotes* claimed that: "when a poor man has too much money, he lends it to the bank; when a rich man hasn't enough, the bank lends it to him". He should have added that the bank lives off the difference in interest rates!

Start-up Financing From Banks

How much money do banks and financial institutions supply to companies that are right at the starting gate? Well, they supply only 9% of such additional funding for incorporated start-ups and 7% of that required by unincorporated start-ups. [Extrapolating figures from *Newly-Formed Small Businesses in Ontario 1982-1984*]

Studies have shown that by far the greatest bulk of initial start-up financing comes from the owners themselves.

The American experience is somewhat similar. A survey suggested that in the United States, banks provided only 14% of the capital required and that most of it (54%) came from personal savings. [*Venture* Magazine, October 1985]

These figures are consistent with the banker's aversion to risk-taking. Banks may be an important source of financing for companies once they are up and running, however, they play a much less significant role at the start-up gate.

In situations where there is no collateral, no receivables, no plant, no real estate and no rich uncles who will guarantee the bank loan, the chances of financing from banks is close to 0% under such circumstances.

If, however, you have personal assets or a spouse who has a steady job, then you may be able to obtain a loan, using personal guarantees. If you can't obtain a business loan, you may at least be able to obtain a personal loan, which in turn, can be used in the business.

Each branch of a bank is a self-contained profit centre which is expected to make money. Since between one quarter and one third of start-up businesses fail within their first two years, start-ups represent a high risk area for the banks to become involved.

It is much easier for a bank to loan money to a business that has been established for many years and has a visible track record than to one that has just appeared out of the blue. In other words, the twinkle in the start-up entrepreneur's eye is unlikely to impress his steely-eyed bank manager.

Banks, generally, are not in the business of supplying unsecured credit or venture capital, however, it should be noted that many large banks operate venture capital subsidiaries, however, almost none of these make investments in start-ups or early stage companies.

It is very difficult for the start-up company to raise financing from banking institutions. This is not said to discourage entrepreneurs, but merely to forewarn them about their chances.

Should the start-up company be at the point of introducing its product to market and shortly be in a position of having inventory and accounts receivable then, it may be possible to arrange an operating line with the bank.

If the start-up requires machinery and assets to commence operation, the banks may be willing to lend part of the money in the form of a term loan; using the equipment or assets as collateral for the loan.

In the case of established companies, bank financing is generally much easier to arrange.

Types of Small Business Loans Offered by Banks

There are a variety of different ways of borrowing money from a bank. The following summarizes some of the more common types of loans and includes many of the "quasi-government" programs that are available. It does not cover direct government loan programs which are dealt with in the volumes in this series on government assistance in each of the ten provinces and two territories.

Operating Lines

Operating lines of credit are used by businesses to provide working capital for their day-to-day operations. This is particularly so when supplier credit and operating cash flow is insufficient to cover the company's need for cash in order to grow.

Basically, an operating line of credit allows the small business owner to borrow funds--as and when required--up to a certain specified limit. Repayment can be made of money not required.

Some bankers like to be involved directly in these transactions; whereas others will allow you to phone in directly to the department that deals with this matter.

The various loans are filled out on a series of pre-signed promissory notes. Your banker will normally request that a whole stack of these be signed when the loan arrangement is entered into.

Some banks have replaced the operating line with an operating account which provides overdraft or line of credit privileges. Interest is calculated daily and deposits made by the business owner are used to automatically draw down the line of credit, thereby reducing interest costs.

139

The interest charged on operating lines is at a premium to the official Bank Rate and usually varies in accordance with it.

As a general guideline, banks are prepared to finance anywhere from 60% to 90% of accounts receivable under 90 days old. This range will vary according to the quality of the receivables but, in practice, will be in the range of 60% - 75%. The figure is often negotiable.

Banks may also grant operating lines on the basis of inventory. Since this is more difficult to dispose of, should things go wrong, it is usually discounted to anywhere between 25% and 50% of its value. If inventory is of a specialized nature without much marketability, the bank may simply not be interested in talking at all.

Theoretically (as in school text books), operating lines may be secured or unsecured. In practice, however, most small businessmen can expect accounts receivable or inventory (or both) to be assigned to the bank and can expect to be required to post personal guarantees as well. In other words, if the business goes sour, the bank may place the business in receivership and collect all the money still owing. If that is insufficient, your "friendly" banker may come pounding on the door and want to sell your house and everything else you have pledged.

It should be pointed out that the bank has the option to "call" the loan at any time and demand immediate payment. This may happen if there is a drop in the value of receivables or inventory to support the loan. It can also happen if the bank manager starts to feel nervous about the company, the economy or any number of things.

Horror stories abound in the small business community about loans that have been "called"; forcing the small business owner (usually at a time when his swamp is already full of alligators) to scuttle around for alternate financing or get his receivables in as fast as possible.

Term Loans

Term loans may be of medium duration - two to seven years; or long term - over seven years. Interest rates may be fixed for the life of the loan at the time it is negotiated. When interest rates are high, there is a tendency for shorter and longer term rates to be much the same. When rates are low, there is a tendency for the banks to want a premium on longer terms. Some term loans may have floating interest rates.

Term loans may be paid off in instalments or in one lump sum at the end. They are generally used to purchase equipment, machinery or fixed assets such as buildings. They may also be used for renovations or expansions.

As a rule of thumb, banks will finance up to about 75% of the amount for buildings based on a recent evaluation. In the case of equipment, it may be 50% of the value or more. You can also expect the assets to be used as collateral for the loan together with the bank's old favourite - the personal guarantee of the business owners.

It should be noted that term lending is not the exclusive domain of the banks. Insurance, trust, acceptance and commercial finance houses are also active in this area.

Floor Plan Loans

Some banks will become involved in floor planning. This is used by manufacturers to finance the goods in the retailer's or distributor's premises. Cars, trucks and seasonal items are frequently financed in this manner. This activity is not confined to banks. Acceptance companies are active in this field.

The arrangement allows the retailer or distributor to stock up on inventory and have it available in time for the commencement of the selling season. He then pays back the loan arranged by the manufacturer as the product is sold.

Warehouse Receipts

Warehouse receipts are frequently used to finance inventories of finished goods and possibly for raw materials. These are normally stored in a public or controlled warehouse and banks (or others) will provide a greater level of financing than if the goods are located on the business owner's premises. Financing of up to 80% of the value of the merchandise or raw materials may be possible.

The rationale behind this type of financing is that the goods or materials are readily marketable and can be readily seized by the creditor in the event of trouble.

Again, this is not an exclusive domain of the banks, however, others in the area are relatively rare. It is suggested that the business owner contact some local public warehouses who may be able to steer him or her in the right direction.

Letters of Credit

A letter of credit is a negotiable document issued by a bank usually to facilitate the purchase of imported or exported goods. These documents are one of the most common methods of payment in international trade.

To illustrate the method of operation, the case of an importer and then an exporter will be examined.

Let us say that you wish to import some goods from XYZ Company. You establish a price with the company and then go to your bank and request that they issue a letter of credit in favour of XYZ Company for the amount in question. This letter states that the bank will honour payment to XYZ Company once the goods are delivered. XYZ Company can then take this letter of credit to its own bank and borrow against it.

Depending on your relationship with your bank, it may not debit your account until the actual payment is made, however, it will probably insist that sufficient funds be maintained in your account, at least to cover the amount in question.

Conversely, let us say that you are exporting to ABC Company. You establish a price for the goods. They go to their bank and have a letter of credit issued in your favour. They send you the letter of credit. You ship the goods and you can take the letter of credit to your bank and you may be able to borrow against it until payment is received.

The bank lends its name to the transaction and guarantees that the supplier will be paid, provided that certain conditions are met. These vary according to the type of letter of credit that is issued and are usually a matter for negotiation between the importer and exporter.

Collateral Required by Banks

Collateral provides the banker with a security net if things go wrong. This is something which every banker will address in the course of preparing his credit review.

It is an area where many start-ups have difficulty. If both the company and the business owner have no assets or other security to offer; the answer to a loan application is almost certain to be negative.

How much is the banker looking for? It depends somewhat on the size of the business. The smaller the business; the greater the proportion of collateral relative to the size of the loan.

A Canadian study found that the average bank collateral demanded of start-ups was 431% (yes - over four times!) of the amount of the loan ["Chartered Bank Financing of Small Business in Canada", University of Western Ontario]. Banks looked to entrepreneurs themselves for most of this amount - 374% from personal assets with the balance from the business

Established businesses fared a little better. Those with sales of under $250,000 required total collateral coverage of 313%.

Those between $1/4 and 1/2 million the coverage was still 251%. Even for companies with sales in excess of $2 million, the coverage was 200%, or double the amount being requested!

A study, released in 1994, by the Canadian Federation of Independent Business found that the average security to loan ratio on business lending was 3.25:1.

It is no wonder that 70% of Canadian business owners complain about excessive collateral demands by the banks!

There is not much alternative; especially if you really need the loan! There are, however, a number of things that can be done to minimize the exposure.

Firstly, negotiate all collateral requirements. Don't just say "yes" and sign the dotted line. Unfortunately, most business owners do this. It is a mistake! Try to negotiate to give up as little as you can.

If the bank is demanding that life insurance policies be signed over to them, make sure that any such amounts are in excess of what has already been arranged for your family in the event of death. In other words, make sure that the bank doesn't get a chance to make your widow or orphans poor!!

A wise move for a business owner who owns a home is to consider transferring registration to a spouse and to try to avoid posting the home as a guarantee. You can bet the bank will want it so they can lay their hands on it if things go sour.

Try and avoid having the spouse co-sign any deal. If you have to, then make sure that you stay on good terms with the spouse!!

The advice of a good lawyer and accountant should be obtained before you sign yourself away to the bank! Remember, the question of guarantees should be a matter of negotiation between the business owner and the banker.

Preparing for A Loan Application

About 80% of the businesspeople who approach a bank for a loan are turned away [Discussion during last program in the series: "Frontrunners", TV Ontario]. This is not because the bank will not loan them money - it is simply because they have not made the preparations to apply for a loan.

The banker needs information; facts and figures: past, present and future. He wants to know how you run your company; who you are; how long you have been at it; how dedicated you are to your business and so on.

Basically, the banker needs to know everything that a well prepared business plan would tell him. In addition to this, he is looking for some specific information which may not have been included in your plan, such as personal information and a personal financial statement.

Your bank manager will want to see a statement of your accounts receivable, which has been aged. In other words, he will want to know the names of the accounts to whom you owe money and how much. He will want these figures on a "current basis" for the past 30 days; for the period 31-60 days; 61-90 days, together with those that are over 90 days.

He may also want to see your accounts payable on the same basis. It may be wise not to offer this information unless it is specifically requested.

A list of inventory will be essential if inventory financing is being sought. It would also be very useful in other circumstances as well.

A schedule of equipment should be prepared; especially if such equipment has any significant value.

In some cases, it may be helpful to have a customer list and even a list of suppliers (which could be useful credit references).

In some instances (especially retail), it could be useful to have a copy of your lease handy - even if it remains in your briefcase during the discussions.

It is a good idea to prepare a financial proposal (in addition to your overall business plan), which shows specifically why you need the money and what you will use it for. Above all, show your banker how he is going to get his money back! Show him your projections and how the loan is to be serviced and paid off.

Include any way of showing your banker how secure the bank's money will be. If there are assets that can be pledged or personal guarantees - then, your task in obtaining a loan will be that much easier. List them so that your manager can see them.

Remember - banks love collateral! They also love guarantees! But also remember that a guarantor of a loan has been described as a fool with a pen in his hand! Guarantees are fine when all is well, but if things go sour - they can come back to haunt the guarantor in the middle of the night! Be careful!

In fairness to the banks, one of the reasons for requesting personal guarantees is to prevent the owners from draining the company of cash by way of excessive salaries or dividends and then leaving the bank with an empty barrel! As you can imagine, the banks have acquired a few empty barrels in their day!

The bank may also reason that, if a business owner is not willing to put his personal assets on the line, then the bank shouldn't bother about putting its assets on the line either.

Make sure that when you borrow - you borrow enough to cover whatever you have in mind. There is nothing worse than finding that you have run out of funds to achieve your objective and that all your assets are tied up as collateral. You could end up having very little room to manoeuvre.

Be open with your banker. Don't hide a lot of dust under the rug - because it is going to come out sooner or later. Every business has its weaknesses and its problems. Don't make these a surprise. Invite him to visit your premises and show him what is going on. Remember that you are selling him on the idea of supporting your business!

Banks love to lend money when the risk is low. It may behove the business owner to borrow from a bank when he does not need the money; just to establish a good credit rating!

When you can show your banker that you don't really need his money, he will come chasing after you with wheelbarrows full of it. Show him that you really need it and he will retire like a tortoise - into his shell! Banks are always willing to lend money to people who don't need it! Indeed, Mark Twain once observed that there are bankers who will loan you an umbrella when the sun is shining but want it back when the rain comes!

Shop for your banker! Look around and enquire in your business community, to find out who the best commercial bankers are in your area.

The best bank is not necessarily the nearest bank!

The best bank manager is the one that understands small business and that you can get along with.

If you end up dealing with a commercial banking branch that is located at a distance from your business; you might consider opening another account with the same bank at a nearby branch to handle your day-to-day deposits and other requirements.

Another clever tactic is to establish both yourself and your business with the bank and get to know them well; especially the manager, months in advance of making any kind of loan application. Have lunch with your bank manager. The nice thing about it is that he will probably want to pay the bill!

Just as in selling, it is harder for somebody to say: "no!", if he likes you and has been doing business with you for a while. Bank managers are human, believe it or not!

Don't forget to ask for an appointment when you want to discuss a loan with your manager. Also, dress well; just as you would when you go to make an important sale.

If the bank says: "no"; ask why your application has been turned down. Listen carefully and if it was for some reason that can be corrected - correct it and try again! Don't give up! If you can't get what you want at one bank, try another! Even within the same banks there are tremendous differences between branches.

Discretionary Limits

Before the small business owner goes charging into his local bank in search of a loan, it may be useful to know that different managers have different ceilings on the amount of money that they are authorized to lend. The banks do not generally advertise these figures and the following information, although a little dated, may be useful.

Assistant managers have discretionary limits of $25,000 to $35,000. Senior Assistant Managers run at about $50,000 and Branch Managers at $100,000. ["Chartered Bank Financing of Small Business In Canada" - University of Western Ontario]

Discretionary limits will also vary according to the size of the branch. The smaller the branch; the lower the limit.

Try to discreetly find out if you are talking to the right person at the bank. If your request is above the limit of the person you are talking to; you may be wasting your time.

The "True" Costs of Borrowing From A Bank

What is all this little exercise going to cost? Well, there are a number of costs; direct and indirect.

Banks have entered the era of the service charge as readers will know from glancing at their daily newspapers! Charges are even being applied for processing loan applications. These fees vary from bank to bank but generally range $100-$200. This is a direct cost.

Another direct cost is the interest charged on the loan or operating line. Generally, it will range anywhere from 0.5% to 3% above the prime lending rate. The average usually lies around 1.5% to 1.6% above prime.

The more risky the loan; the higher the premium that will be charged.

There are also indirect costs. These are the potential costs to the company and to the owner in the event that things go wrong. They can be tremendously high.

Many a small business owner has lost his home and practically everything else that he owned to a bank. This is a sobering thought which should be considered carefully before dashing into a bank for money.

Giving up some ownership in the company, in the form of equity, might end up being much cheaper in the long run than borrowing from a bank!

Factoring As A Method of Borrowing

Factoring is not commonly used for business financing. This was revealed in a 1985 survey conducted by Dun & Bradstreet on 1,060 American companies. It found that only 7% used factoring as a means of financing. It tends to be used a lot in the garment industry.

Financing of accounts receivable was discussed earlier in this chapter. Under that arrangement, the receivables were assigned to the bank but actually remained the property of the small business. This would continue, so long as the bank was satisfied with the relationship. Should it fall apart, the bank has the right by law to go to the company's customers and collect the monies owing directly.

In the case of factoring, the business sells its accounts receivable to a third party - known as a "factor". The latter takes on the responsibility of collecting the money owing.

The factoring company assumes the risk that the customer will pay his bill.

If the customer fails to pay after a specified period of time (usually 90 days); the factor pays the small business or credits its account even though the factor has not received payment.

Obviously, the factoring company will examine the credit of the small business's customers very closely and if the credit is not satisfactory, may refuse to factor those particular accounts. The small business is still free to sell to such accounts at its own risk.

In practice, the small business will perform a credit check (through the factor) on the customer to ensure that the credit standing is satisfactory even before the goods are shipped and invoiced. This reduces the possibility of the factor refusing to accept certain invoices.

In order to reduce risks, factors will maintain credit checking operations; together with their own collection facilities. This is the biggest advantage factors offer since many small businesses do not have the staff or the time to do this on their own. Collecting on overdue bills is also a very time consuming and unpleasant task.

Methods of Payment

There are two methods by which the customer can pay for the goods received from the small business.

The first, is direct payment to the factor. Basically, the small business informs its customer that payment should be made directly to the factor.

Under the second, payment is still made to the small business, which then endorses the cheques in favour of the factor. Some endorsements are carefully camouflaged to prevent customers from knowing they are actually paying their bills to a factor.

Method of Financing

There are two steps in factoring. The first, is the element of factoring itself. The second, is the borrowing of funds against the accounts that have been factored.

The first step is for the factor to collect on the monies owing. Normal trade credit is for 30 days, although many customers attempt to stretch this out for longer. When a customer makes payment, the factor credits the small business with the amount less its factoring fee. This fee normally ranges between 1% and 3%.

For argument's sake, assume that the fee is 2% and the invoice is for $1,000. When payment is received, $980 ($1,000 less 2%) is credited to the small business account. If for any reason, the customer fails to pay, the factor will still credit the small business account after a specified period of time; usually 90 days. In the above example, the $980 would be credited and the factoring company would absorb the loss.

The fee which the factor charges is obviously a function of the quality of the accounts of the small business; their size and the volume of business. Should the small business leave the funds with the factor beyond the period when they were collected, interest would be paid on the monies in the account.

The second step involves borrowing against the invoices which have been sold to the factor. The borrowing can be for a higher percentage of the receivables than offered by the banks. Thus, a factor will frequently lend money against 90% of the value of the receivables, as opposed to the 60% to 75% normally offered by the banks.

The factor will hold 10% in reserve.

In the above example, the small business would be entitled to borrow up to an additional 90% of the $1,000 from the factor. The interest charged for such borrowing is usually 2% to 3% above prime. The amount of this interest is usually deducted in calculating the cash advance. The arithmetic on the example is as follows:

```
Invoice amount                          $1,000.00
Reserve (10%)                              100.00
Factor's fee (2%)                           20.00
Interest $880 @ 14% x 45 days               15.19
Cash Advance                               864.81
Release of Reserve after payment           100.00
Total finally realized from sale           964.81
```

In this example, the total factoring cost to the small business is about 3.5% over the 45 day period; or about 28.5% on an annualized basis. In looking at these figures one must remember that the factor is assuming all the risk - as opposed to the banks which assume no risk!

Advantages and Disadvantages of Factoring

The big advantage of factoring for the small business is the credit checking facility. The factor is set up to perform large numbers of credit checks and has the staff and resources to do it properly. This function can be time consuming for the small business and subject to errors; especially if staff are careless in conducting checks. Another big advantage is that the small business is always going to receive its money. If the customer does not pay, that becomes the factor's problem for collection.

Factoring provides the small business with immediate cash when the sale is made. The business does not have to wait until the customer decides to pull his cheque book out of the drawer and write up a cheque. The amount of cash advanced by a factor against receivables is likely to be higher than that offered by the banks.

The big disadvantage of factoring is the cost! The factor is in the business to make money and the business owner has to pay for the advantages that the factor has to offer. Another disadvantage is that factoring may affect your relationship with your bank for other borrowing. Consultation with your banker would be advisable before any agreement is reached.

Some customers attach stigma against small businesses using a factor, especially when payments must be made directly to the factor. Customers may question the financial stability of businesses using factors, even if such fears are totally unfounded.

Who Can Factor

As previously mentioned, factoring started in the garment and textile industries. It is now accepted in a much wider variety of business activities such as wholesale, manufacturing, building supply, etc.

Where to Find Factors

The simplest way of finding factors is to consult the yellow pages of any major city.

Leasing As A Form of Debt Financing

Leasing is one method of small business financing, especially in the area of vehicles, computers and office equipment.

Leasing in Canada has gained tremendous popularity within the last few years and now accounts for 10% to 12% of all new equipment purchases; up from 4% just a few years ago.

According to the Equipment Leasors Association of Canada, leasing in Canada still lags far behind the United States where it accounts for 25% to 30% of all new equipment purchases.

Under a leasing arrangement, the leasing company owns the asset. The small business gets to use the asset for a monthly or quarterly charge. There are three basic varieties of the leasing arrangement.

The first type of arrangement

In one type, the business does not build up any equity in the equipment leased. At the end of a lease, the asset is simply returned to the leasing company which then disposes of it.

This arrangement is known as a "fixed-in lease", "closed-end lease", "walk-away lease", "operating lease" or "net lease".

Because of the leasing company's responsibility to dispose of the asset, it is exposed to the risk that the asset will be mistreated whilst it is being leased. For this reason, some leasing companies charge more to compensate for any losses.

In cases of excessive abuse, the leasing company may require extra payment to compensate for reduced value.

Such leases for vehicles are likely to contain a stipulation relating to the number of kilometres that can be driven. Any amounts over the maximum will be subject to an extra charge on a per kilometre basis. This can be expensive to the business leasing the vehicle, if the limits are greatly exceeded.

It is also difficult to get out of this type of lease before its termination date.

The second type of arrangement

Another type of lease allows the business to build up equity ownership in the equipment leased.

At the end of the lease, the asset is sold either to the business or to a third party for a pre-determined amount known as the "buy-back".

This type of lease is known as an "open-end lease", "buy-back lease", "capital lease" or "financed lease".

The party entering into the lease guarantees this final price. If the asset is sold for less than the buy-back price, then the small business must make up the difference. If it is sold for more, the profit goes into the business (where it may be subject to tax - check with your accountant).

This type of lease is usually fairly easy to get out of before it expires. The "buy-back" is simply calculated at any given point in time in accordance with a pre-determined schedule. Most leasing periods are for between 12 and 48 months; although other periods exist on the market.

In the case of these "open-end leases", it is frequently possible to obtain lease extensions which essentially reduce the ultimate buy-back price.

The third type of arrangement

There are hybrid leases which combine some of the features of both "open" and "closed-end" leases.

Maintenance and repair

Maintenance and repair of the equipment can either be the responsibility of the leasing company or the responsibility of the small business.

In most car leases, the small business would be responsible for maintenance and repairs.

For office equipment such as typewriters, photocopiers, etc., the leasing company will frequently take responsibility for the repair and maintenance. In the latter case, a maintenance charge is added to the basic lease rates.

It should be noted that full-service leases for vehicles are becoming more widely available in North America. Some of these are not directly tied into the lease and can be entered into separately. Thus, one of the major oil companies in Canada is offering a fleet program, which in reality is only a semi-maintenance program. This allows for discounts on parts and gas; includes warranties on maintenance work; provides all the billing information and eliminates unauthorized purchases by employees.

Insurance

In some instances (especially with vehicles), the business will be required to carry insurance on the asset.

Some leasing companies offer insurance as part of their service to the customer, however, the rates may or may not be competitive.

The Leasing Company's Viewpoint

The leasing company owns the asset and is able to use the capital cost allowance for tax purposes. It also charges the small business interest for the money that is tied up in the asset.

Should the business fail or stop making lease payments; the leasing company will simply come in and remove the equipment which legally belongs to it. At that point, their risk is reduced to the difference between the price that they can obtain when they sell the used equipment and the amount of principal still outstanding on the lease.

It is for this reason that the leasing company prefers to lease equipment that will have a marketable value in the event of something going wrong. Therefore, the business owner, may find leasing companies reluctant to enter into agreements involving high technology products which may become obsolete very quickly.

Advantages of Leasing

There are a number of advantages of leasing for the small business.

Firstly, it helps to conserve working capital. The company does not have to lay out cash for the outright purchase of the asset and can use those funds for day-to-day expenses and operations.

Comparing leasing to equipment purchased on a financing plan; payments are generally lower under the leasing arrangement. Also, most leases cover 100% of the equipment cost, including delivery, which is unlikely to be the case under a financing plan.

Secondly, leasing does not affect a firm's ability to borrow from its bank or other sources. The lease does not tie up any assets as collateral, simply because the asset does not legally belong to the business in the first place.

Thirdly, businesses can charge lease payments as operating expenses; thereby reducing taxes more than would have been possible by claiming capital cost allowances (under normal circumstances). Term of leases can also be geared to life expectancy of equipment.

Interest rates charged on leases are usually fixed at the time they are entered into. A business knows exactly in advance what its cost is going to be. This can be an advantage if the lease is signed at a time of low interest rates; because the rate is locked in. The converse is true at times of high interest rates.

Some leases are available with floating rates, however, these are less common.

An advantage, touted by leasing companies, is protection against obsolescence. In this high tech era, many pieces of equipment become rapidly outdated. Leasing permits trading up to a new piece of equipment; thereby keeping an edge over competitors.

Leasing allows a business to make equipment "sing for its supper", or pay its own way. The additional monthly revenue generated from the use of a new piece of leased equipment will frequently exceed the monthly leasing charges.

In the case of automobiles, some big leasing companies have such enormous buying power that it permits them to obtain discounts that can be passed on to their customers.

Leasing is usually available, even in poor economic times, to small businesses with good credit ratings. This may not necessarily be the case with bank loans, which can become as scarce as hen's teeth when the economy is falling out of the sky and your bank manager is hiding under his desk!

Disadvantages of Leasing

If leasing is so wonderful, why isn't everyone using it? Well, it certainly has gained a tremendous amount of popularity over the last 20 years. In fact leasing in North America is now a multi-billion business. There are, however, some disadvantages.

The first is cost. The leasing company is not doing it for free and charges interest on the money that is tied up in the asset.

The second is that, unless there is a buy-back provision at the end of the lease, the business will relinquish the equipment on termination of the lease and have nothing to show for it after all those payments!

On the other hand, if there is a buy-back, the equipment may fall short of the buy-back price when it is sold and the business will be held liable for the difference. This could happen in the case of a vehicle which has been poorly maintained or has clocked up a very large number of miles or kilometres.

In the case of a closed end lease, a vehicle which has exceeded the pre-set mileage limit will be subject to a surcharge based on a per kilometre usage. If the equipment is in poor condition, the leasing company may demand compensation to make up for the lower resale price. This can be a source of considerable irritation to both parties.

Under a lease, the business does not own the asset, so it cannot be used as collateral for any other form of borrowing.

It is easy to get caught up in the sales talk about wanting to avoid obsolescence. Is a talking photocopier better than one that does not talk? Is there really any very significant competitive advantage in having the latest this or that?

If you lease at a fixed rate when rates are high - you may be stuck until the lease expires. This would not be the case with a loan which has floating interest rates. On the other hand, leases do exist which carry floating interest rates.

The Lease or Purchase Decision

To come to a decision as to whether to lease or purchase a particular piece of equipment, the business owner must weigh the pros and cons.

If the small business has plenty of cash, leasing may not make sense because of the interest charges. On the other hand, if cash is tight, leasing makes a lot of sense.

In some cyclical types of businesses (where the cycles are of one or two year durations), leasing could be advantageous. Such might apply to a company with a major contract for a specified period of time or a certain project that will have a finite length. Staff and equipment may only be needed for a one or two year period.

Monthly payments on a lease may be less than installment payments for a loan. This is particularly so for cars and trucks. The lease payments are based on the difference between the projected wholesale value at the end of the lease and the initial value. In the case of installment payments, the full value of the equipment has to be paid off.

To counter this advantage which leasing has over borrowing, some banks have introduced a guaranteed buy-back value for vehicles.

Under this arrangement, the banks simply finance the difference between the purchase price of the vehicle and the guaranteed buy-back price. Since this price spread is smaller, the monthly payments are correspondingly smaller. There is, however, a small interest premium that has to be paid in order to enjoy this privilege.

Frequently a loan will require a certain percentage down payment in advance e.g., 20%. A lease frequently requires only an initial cash layout for the first and last month's payments.

In some instances, two months payments are required by way of deposit. Incidentally, no interest is paid on lease deposits. Personal guarantees may also be requested, especially for small companies or those at the start-up stage.

In coming to a final decision, it would be wise to consult an accountant or other professional who can provide some unbiased advice, especially with regard to the "real" benefits to the business and to the "true" costs after taxes are taken into account.

14

CASH MANAGEMENT

What is Cash Management?

Cash management is the most important aspect of successful bootstrap financing. It involves the management of money in relation to time. The faster money comes in; the slower it goes out and what you do with it during the time that you have it in your hands are the key ingredients of cash management. It is a disciplined approach to controlling cash flow.

Many banks are now offering cash management services. Some of these are geared towards small business and entrepreneurs are advised to investigate their application to their particular situation.

A review of cash management in relation to small business should focus on four areas, as follows.

Accounts Receivable

Accounts receivable is the money owing to you by customers. Most manufacturing companies offer trade terms to their customers. These are frequently of 30 days duration. If you don't offer it - you may not get the business, however, you should try and get this money in as fast as you can.

In most retail types of business - it's cash on the barrel, unless credit cards are used; in which case the cash is being discounted by the amount that the card company charges the merchant for the transaction. At least the merchant obtains his money quickly.

In many other types of business, however, this is not so and the offering of trade credit is an accepted practice.

The most obvious precaution is to make sure that the invoice is mailed very promptly as soon as the goods are shipped. An invoice that goes out late gets into the "pile" of payables late at the other end and the chances are that it also gets paid late.

Another technique is to send out monthly statements. These are a nuisance to prepare but they do serve as a constant reminder to the customer that an amount is still owing.

One suggestion for encouraging prompt payment is to offer prompt payment discounts. If you have enough room in your product pricing, these can built in to start with.

Make sure that your invoice is designed in such a way that the discount is obvious to anyone who reads it. Thus, you could offer terms of "2% 10 days/Net 30 days".

Discounts will encourage some accounts to pay promptly but don't expect your mail box to be bursting with cheques as soon as you introduce the scheme.

166

Depending on the type of customer you are catering to, it is possible that only a small portion will take you up on your generosity.

To further encourage prompt payment, you could increase the discount. You can only do this if your profit margin will comfortably allow it.

Don't forget that a 5% discount for payment in 10 days is equivalent to 5% interest on the money up to the time it was due anyway (30 days in this case). If the cheque is received in 10 days then you are paying 5% interest for the privilege of having the money 20 days early.

Working this 5% discount out, you will see that you are paying 91% interest on an annualized basis! You can bet that banks certainly don't offer that on savings accounts! Even a 2% discount for payment in 10 days/net 30, is still worth 36% on an annualized basis!

Of course, there are several catches in this argument.

Firstly, the cheque from the customer taking advantage of the discount frequently takes more than 10 days to arrive.

Secondly, it is a rare customer that pays promptly in 30 days when the bill is due.

The only way to calculate the real cost of offering such a discount is to find out the average length of time that it takes to receive your money - say 45 days and to subtract the average length of time it takes the prompt payment discount cheques to arrive - say 15 days. In the above examples you would be paying 2% or 5% for having money 30 days early - still equivalent to 24% and 61% annually.

If you continue this argument and assume that payment does not come in for 65 days on a "2% 10/net 30" invoice with 15 days being the average period for discount takers; then money only costs less than 15% - still higher than bank rates but much closer to them.

If the money does not come in for 90 days, then the cost would be only 9.7% - closer to what it might cost you to borrow from the bank.

These examples illustrate that prompt payment discounting can be expensive money, depending on the length of time involved to collect on receivables. If a company can collect on "net 30" in less than 60 days, it would almost be better to go to a bank and borrow against accounts receivables on a prime plus basis, rather than offer any prompt payment discount. It really depends how desperate the business is for cash.

The converse of prompt payment discounts is to charge late payment interest penalties. Thus, for every day that an account is overdue, interest is tacked onto the total and presented in the monthly statement as a separate charge.

Care has to be taken not to antagonize the account by charging too much interest or by being too insistent that such interest actually be paid. Customers can be lost in this way and some diplomacy may be called for. Discretion is sometimes the better part of valour!

It may be better to have a regular customer that pays a little late than lose the customer altogether. Be warned, however, that many customers just pay late because they know they can get away with it. It is best to start off by showing them the rules according to your game. Be firm but diplomatic!

Try every ruse you can to ensure that money comes in as fast as possible. Companies that supply their customers on a regular basis have the advantage of insisting that overdue invoices be paid before more product is shipped.

Suppliers who are selling to a new customer, on a "once only" basis (i.e., they don't expect repeat orders), have the advantage that shipment will only be made cash on delivery (COD) because of the time and expense involved in performing credit checks for just one shipment.

Equally, companies that are supplying things on a custom-made basis, such as customized displays, may have justification for asking the customer for a deposit with his order - at least enough to cover the cost of the materials and possibly more.

Some companies have started to request a 50% payment with orders. This is fine, if customers go along with it, however, most industrial companies like and indeed, expect to be offered traditional trade credit.

Contractors commonly ask for payments on a performance basis.

An important aspect of receivables management is to check a customer's credit rating before any business dealings commence.

New customers should be required to fill out a credit application form and no shipments made until the credit references are checked.

You can perform your own credit checks. There are also reporting agencies, such as Dun and Bradstreet, who will supply credit information on a fee basis.

Make sure that credit information is kept current. A good customer one year can turn into a bad customer the next, depending on economic or other conditions.

Some businesses are very cyclical - this is true of many retailers, many of whom do as much as 90% of their annual business over the Christmas period.

Credit limits should be established according to the credit rating of the customer. High risk customers should be accorded a low limit - say $1,000. If they want to purchase more than that - the excess must be COD.

Overdue accounts should be reminded of that fact about a couple of weeks after payment is due. Make sure that the right person is contacted - usually the clerk in charge of payables.

At the early stages, it is customary to do this by mail with a polite letter or reminder. Gentle persuasion should start after 45 days on a net 30 invoice. Once the account is over 60 days, it is suggested that the telephone be used together with mail on a weekly basis.

Be firm, when you use the phone! Suggest to the customer that you will send a courier to pick up the cheque or suggest that your sales representative will come round to pick it up.

If the customer says that the cheque will be ready on Wednesday - call on Wednesday to make sure and have someone pick it up right away. An overnight courier can save a lot of aggravation. It is surprising how many companies use the excuse that cheques are "in the mail!" Having a courier pick up the cheque at your expense, can eliminate that excuse.

Businesses with a lot of incoming cheques from across the country, may want to consider a lockbox arrangement with a bank.

The lockbox allows the cheque to be mailed to a box address in the customer's area which is operated by the bank. This ensures prompt depositing by reducing the time in the mail.

Lockbox techniques may speed up the rate of depositing by as much as four to ten days. The volume of business, however, would have to be reasonable to justify the costs of such an arrangement.

Once the account goes over 90 days, you've got a problem!

The most important precaution is to try to ensure that you minimize the number of seriously overdue accounts. If you do get stuck, try to get the customer to agree to a partial payment plan and stay on top of it. Failing that, threaten to sue!

It is sometimes better to allow a collection agency to handle the matter instead of spending hours sitting around in small claims courts. This is particularly true if the account is located far away.

Collection agencies are not cheap and you may end up having to give away as much as 50% of the amount owing - but then half a loaf is better than none! But remember that collection agencies have very little magic that you cannot apply yourself. Quite often they will also come up empty handed.

Setting up a system to control receivables is essential to good cash management. Make sure that credit checks are performed; overdue accounts are contacted on a regular basis and that as much effort goes into collecting the money, as in selling the product.

All the sales efforts are wasted if the customer does not pay and it can cost a lot if he is slow in paying. The best time to start is at the beginning. Once a customer knows he can get away with slow payment he will try to take advantage of you. Be firm!

Even if you can reduce the average outstanding period of your receivables (assuming no discounts) by as little as 10 days on monthly sales of $100,000; you will self-finance yourself to the tune of over $30,000. Think about it!

Accounts Payable

Accounts payable are the amounts of money owed to your suppliers or to any other party. Here, the shoe is on the other foot. It's time to sit on the other side of the fence. Reverse everything that was said above!

Initially, many entrepreneurs may not have to face this problem, since many suppliers do not issue trade credit to start-ups unless they can supply good credit references. Start-ups frequently find themselves on COD terms until they can prove themselves.

The secret to accounts payable financing is to either accept any attractive prompt payment discounts (as discussed above) or to maximize on the float time. The latter requires skill and care. Accounts that are 90 days or older frequently become COD on the next order. A bad credit rating can seriously affect a firm's ability to survive.

The key is to stretch, but not overdo it! A good credit rating is worth far more than one "stretch", that went too far.

It is especially important for a new business to establish a good credit rating as soon as possible. Prompt payment of bills should take priority, so that good credit references are established. The ready availability of credit to a new business is far more important than trying to squeeze a few more days out of a payable.

Don't overlook negotiating with your suppliers for the best price possible, based on yearly sales volume. Some companies will accept an order for a large quantity of merchandise which can be shipped at so many units per month or even better - only shipped on an "as needed" basis. Such techniques may permit you to take advantage of volume price discounts.

Another technique is to arrange the longest terms possible with your supplier. If you are a large customer, you may be successful in obtaining extended terms. It is worth a try - don't forget he wants your business!

Cash Balances

Banks got away with murder when they pay no interest on small business current accounts. Those days are happily coming to an end, as other financial institutions offer daily interest - some even as high as term deposit rates over certain minimum balances. This is causing some banks to reluctantly follow suit, but I suspect that they are attempting to make up for it through increased service charges!

Consolidation of the funds from various bank accounts into one account will frequently enable a company to obtain higher interest rates or permit it to purchase term deposits, GICs or T-Bills. To obtain the best rates, it is advisable to shop the money markets. Such purchases will have to take into account the maturities and should be the subject of cash budgeting in advance.

Foreign exchange losses can play havoc with profits.

Take the case of United States based companies, which are selling into foreign markets whose currencies have declined in value relative to the American dollar. Assuming that their products or services are sold in the local currency (to remain competitive with local suppliers) then the profits will be less in value when they are repatriated to the United States.

If a Canadian business person orders something from the United States and the Canadian Dollar decides to sink to the bottom of the sea (as it did a number of years ago), before the bill is paid, the product may end up costing a lot more than expected.

The only way to counteract these types of potential losses is through currency hedging. Thus the Canadian purchaser can opening up a US Dollar account. Place enough funds into it at the time the order is placed to cover the bill.

One last piece of advice; with all the bank, trust, savings and loan failures that have taken place - make sure that the financial institution is safe. Deposit insurance is one thing but the amount of time it may take you to regain your money may put your business in serious jeopardy.

Inventory Management

Inventory is like cash. Make sure it works for you!

If excess inventory sits idle - it is like having excess cash at the bank in a non-interest paying account. You cannot sell from an empty wagon, however, this should not preclude you from paring down excess inventory to the minimum level necessary to support your customers.

There are three key ingredients in successful inventory management.

The first is knowing the minimum amount of inventory you require to support your day-to-day operations; whilst at the same time, maintaining a small buffer for unexpected requirements. This requires a study of your historical sales patterns and projections of your future requirements.

It is essential that you maintain enough inventory to satisfy your customer's needs or for your own production requirements, however, any excess should be eliminated. Calculating this can be very laborious work; but fortunately computers have come to the rescue and can reduce a lot of the time and paperwork. The cost of computerization for inventory control will often pay for itself in surprisingly short periods of time.

The second is knowing how long it takes the supplier to deliver and whether the supplier maintains sufficient inventory for you to draw on.

The ideal scenario is to have your supplier next door with lots of stock. Every time you receive an order you rush next door, buy some more product and ship it under your name!

The disaster scenario is to have to wait three months for the product to arrive from the Orient, on top of another three months for the next factory run!

The third factor is to ensure that purchases are made in economical quantities. Quantity discounts and declining unit freight costs are two critical determinants in the purchasing decision. Such savings have to be weighed against the cost of carrying the extra inventory and the amount of money that will be tied up in the process.

A factor to be considered by the manufacturing operation is inventory of work in progress. Good scheduling is required to ensure that when a product starts to be produced; it goes through production from one process directly to the next without sitting around for ages. This cuts down on inventory requirements.

Another consideration for the manufacturer, is to calculate and schedule material requirements. If a particular product is not going to be produced for six months; then there is no need to carry an inventory of parts until the start of production.

In the case of retailers, proper inventory information can permit the elimination of slow moving lines and allow for increased emphasis on best-sellers.

Computers linked to cash register systems now make perpetual inventory systems a reality. The costs of such systems are declining rapidly and the benefits can be quite spectacular. Retailers who can reduce (or eliminate) excess inventories of slow moving items can end up saving a bundle.

The ideal scenario for a retailer is to have just enough inventory to satisfy the needs of customers during that day, week or month; with one extra left on the shelf at the end of that period for show (or the impulse sale!).

Computers will not perform the task of a crystal ball but they will tell the retailer what has happened historically and provide some insight into what his future requirements will be on an item-by-item basis.

It is then up to the retailer to correctly judge delivery times and to make sure that adantage is taken of quantity discounts where these may be favourable. Care has also to be taken to judge the level of buffer stock, to ensure he retains his customer base. It's a sad day when a hamburger restaurant runs out of hamburger buns! On the other hand, it might get away with running out of some of the "fixings".

15

COST CONTROL

The Importance of Cost Control

The second most important factor in bootstrap financing is that of controlling internal costs. It is easy to let the costs of doing business creep up, when things are going well. Such incremental increases can reduce the amount of money a firm has at its disposal for internal financing.

It is not the purpose of this book to discuss all the factors involved in cost control analysis; but to point out some of the more obvious ones and to stimulate discussion.

The control of costs requires the cooperation of all the employees in a company. It is no use for the president to switch the lights off in his office in the evening, if the employees leave the lights burning in an empty plant all night!

What may be good for one company; may have no application in another. The text that follows suggests some areas that might be worthy of consideration.

Energy Costs

An analysis of energy costs should include a look at sources of possible loss. Is there sufficient insulation? Would double glazing cut down on energy costs?

The author has been amazed at the number of shipping doors that are not properly protected during the winter. An employee who steals $100 in cash would likely be fired. Yet, if that same employee lets $100 of heat out through a shipping door into the cold winter air outside, probably no-one would say anything about it! Even managers who are aware that screens exist that can be placed over some doors do little about it!

Going to the other extreme, spot lights in a retail environment can generate so much heat that air conditioning has to be kept on even during winter months! Such "double" energy costs can be reduced by installing some of the new lighting systems which cut back dramatically on the amount of energy used. The only way to determine their usefulness in any particular situation is to perform a cost benefit analysis.

Devices are now available that can be attached to fluorescent lighting circuits that will reduce energy consumed by as much as 50%. According to a Canadian report, lighting costs account for about 18% of operating expenses in the industrial environment and the installation of such devices can lead to significant savings. [*Canadian Business*, November 1985]

What is the best form of heating energy to use - oil; electricity; gas? What is the best form of energy for vehicles - gas, propane, diesel or battery? Are there any significant cost advantages in changing?

If heat is generated during an industrial process - can it be recycled or put to other use?

Is the heat turned down at night when the plant is vacant?

Computerized timing devices are now available that will turn heating up in the morning to optimum temperatures just before employees start to arrive. These devices will automatically turn temperatures down before quitting time in the evening. Some such systems are very expensive; whereas others can now be run off inexpensive personal computers. The same equipment can control air conditioning units in the summer.

A company is never too small to benefit from an analysis of its energy consumption. Implementing some small changes can often uncover hidden amounts of cash!

Transportation Costs

In the age of "zero inventory"; air freight has considerable merits. The added cost, however, must be measured against the benefits.

Pooling of shipments and co-op shipping can reduce both incoming and outgoing freight costs, however, such services; while fairly common in the United States; are only available on a limited basis in Canada. [*Toronto Business*, February 1984]

Travel Costs

It is claimed that travel expenses are the third largest expense of Canadian businesses. [Business and Finance, October 1984]

The use of a wise corporate travel agent or one of the new breed of "management travel consultants" would be a good place to start. Such people should be able to answer a number of basic travel questions: is the maximum advantage being taken from "seat sales"? from advanced booking discounts? Many hotels offer "corporate rates" which can lead to significant discounts.

Make sure that controls are in place to monitor travelling expenses by employees.

The use of corporate credit cards can increase cash float simply because of the delays in billing time. Such cards also reduce the quantities of paperwork and eliminate the necessity of laying out cash advances for travel. The downfall of such cards is possible abuse by employees and consequently, liability for misuse should be established before such cards are issued.

Question whether trips are necessary in the first place. Would a conference call, fax, e-mail or letter achieve the same result at much less cost?

Communication Costs

Anyone who watches television will have been bombarded with telephone company commercials extolling the virtues of a device invented by Alexander Graham Bell. Whether the good gentleman would have approved of all the uses of his invention is another matter!

Teleconferencing can significantly reduce travel costs and more importantly, travel time.

Small companies without fancy teleconferencing equipment can simply dial "0" and request the conference call operator. The operator, in turn, can connect the necessary parties to the conversation. Video can also be added to such conferencing but is an expensive and often unnecessary luxury, since it involves the use of a special studio.

Telemarketing can be used to solicit orders (especially repeat orders) from customers over the phone. It can be used to generate sales leads and qualify them before a sales representative makes a call; thereby helping the rep to utilize time in the best possible way.

Telemarketing can also be used to follow up on sales leads. Remember that the average cost of a personalized industrial sales visit is in excess of $200. This would include the salesperson's time, salary, travel and other expenses. Theses costs are constantly rising. Anything that can be done to make the calling more cost effective is worth it.

The telephone can be very effective in assisting the collection of accounts receivable. It has many uses - but it is also an expensive beast!

To reduce costs, consider limiting the number of phones from which long distance calls can be made. Instal a system whereby long distance calling will be logged according to phone extension.

To be effective, conference calls and sales calls should be well planned. WATS and IN-WATS lines may cut down on costs.

Most companies now use Fax machines. These devices help to cut down on the "gab" time which is so typical of regular phone conversations. They can also provide a more accurate record for later referral because the exchange is down on paper which avoids anyone saying: "that isn't what I said!".

Communication between computers - "electronic mail" or e-mail is now widely used and is very inexpensive (especially for out-of-town and overseas communications), since it usually comes as part of the package offered by Internet Service Providers (ISPs). The device that makes such communication possible over a phone line is a modem. The use of e-mail helps to reduce costs and leaves more cash available for other purposes.

The Internet also permits voice communication and rather poor quality video-conferencing. As bandwidths and technology improve, Internet communications will greatly improve in years to come.

Advertising Costs

Analyzing responses from advertising programs can be a very inexact and exasperating task. There may be days when business owners wonder if advertising is really worth it.

One of the major soft drinks companies once decided to abandon its use of general advertising and you guessed it - sales dropped!

The only way to ascertain which advertising medium is the most suitable for you is to try it and attempt to analyze the results. To do this effectively, attribute each sale to something: did it result from a trade show? a piece of direct mail? the yellow pages? an advertisement?

Such an analysis may be easier to perform in a manufacturing environment where sales reps can record the source of the lead. In retail, it may only be possible to monitor results in relation to specific products that are advertised.

Once you have the sales results - compare them with the costs of that advertising medium. Calculate the advertising cost per dollar of sale generated.

Such an analysis can be very revealing and can assist in cutting out unnecessary advertising expenses. This, in turn, can assist in generating internal cash or reallocating money to more productive areas.

Employee Costs

One of the largest expenses in small business is usually that relating to employees. These costs come in a number of guises.

Firstly, there are the obvious direct costs of both payroll and benefits. Paying employees every two weeks instead of every week can help create temporary increases in cash float. Deferring benefits - such as a bonus to year end can also assist.

Offering employees shares in the company through employee stock ownership plans can reduce cash outlays, although these usually come in the form of a "bonus" or an extra "carrot" for working with the company. Such plans have the added advantage of greatly increasing employee motivation to make a company successful and were discussed earlier in this book.

Small businesses are at a distinct disadvantage when it comes to "benefit packages" and job security, when compared to larger corporations. Very few small firms offer dental and pension plans. They may, therefore, have to pay a premium in order to attract the best employees.

The premiums could be in the form of profit sharing (which creates a drain on available cash) or share purchase options (which don't).

On the other hand, a report has suggested that there was little acceptance of incentives based on employee performance in small business [*INC Magazine*, September 1984]. This was attributed to the close working relationship between owner and staff.

Then, there are indirect costs. Training new employees can be expensive and high turnover may prove to be more costly in the long run that the paying of higher wages to attract and retain the "right" people.

Poor employee morale can have devastating indirect costs. Customers can be turned off by sulky or indifferent employees and quality of workmanship can deteriorate. Improved communication between owners and employees can help alleviate some of these morale problems.

Subcontracting

Subcontracting can prove to be an effective method of cutting costs in certain instances. This is particularly the case when the volume of work is insufficient to justify full-time employment of a skilled person; or where expensive equipment is required in the preparation of an item.

Subcontracting can be used with everything, from bookkeeping to metal cutting; from silk screening to injection moulding. In fact, subcontracting is very common in small business.

The unit costs of subcontracting may be higher than performing the task internally; but the overall savings in not having to have a skilled person permanently on the payroll could be greater; assuming that the job is intermittent in nature.

In many instances, there may actually be savings in subcontracting. The subcontractor may have sophisticated equipment that will perform the task much faster.

An example might be a firm selling Masonite that will cut-to-size for their customers. They may operate saws that will cut a large number of sheets at one time which could make the job much cheaper than doing it in-house on a sheet-by-sheet basis.

Because a subcontractor is being paid premium rates, productivity is often (but not always) higher. An added bonus may be better quality of work and accuracy.

The converse of the above argument is - do you have any idle equipment time that could be used to subcontract to others? If so, could this generate added revenue?

Computerization

Computers were here long before Time Magazine ran a computer on its front cover as "Man of the Year". The difference is that they are now a lot less expensive and will do a great deal more.

Factory Automation

Following initial successes in Japan; factory automation and robotics are gaining ever increasing toe-holds in North America. The cost of much of this technology is decreasing; whilst the software and sophistication is increasing. Many systems are now being designed for smaller business applications.

This technology can prove very cost effective. Labour costs can be significantly reduced and quality greatly improved.

Automation will be the largest component of effective cost cutting in North American industry during the next decade. The survival of many small businesses will depend on their willingness to adopt these new technologies.

Quality Control

The production of defective goods can lead to a significant drain of cash for a small business.

There are the direct costs associated with producing defective items - the materials and time wasted. Time delays caused by re-runs may cause deadlines to be missed and possibly to order cancellations.

If the defect is not spotted and goods are shipped; there are indirect costs in the form of customer dissatisfaction and reduced sales.

If products are sold under warranty; there can be substantial costs associated with fulfilling commitments made under those warranty provisions.

An illustration of the cost associated with poor quality of production can be obtained by taking an extreme example. If half the items in a production run are defective; then the cost of producing the other half is likely to be double; unless parts from the defective items can be reclaimed.

Components used in production should be inspected when they arrive to insure that they are up to standard. There is nothing worse than opening a box on the day of a scheduled production run to find that incoming materials are defective!

Quality control starts with an inspection of the quality of every piece of material when it comes in and certainly well before it is used in production.

One of the advantages of utilizing robots and automated systems with built-in quality control monitors, is a consistency of output which may not be possible with human operators.

Waste Management

The right kind of trash can be turned into cash. This is particularly true for metal scrap, fabrics, oil, chemicals, etc. Some of these materials can be re-cycled or they can be sold outright to dealers for cash.

Theft and Shrinkage

A significant business cost; especially for retailers, is that of shrinkage. The Retail Council of Canada suggested that the median shrinkage rate in Canada is about

1.4%. In certain types of stores, the figures were much higher. Thus, 10% of all stores that were surveyed reported shrinkage in excess of 3%. A tenth of the pharmacies surveyed reported shrinkage of over 5% and for toy stores it was 4%.

Whilst much of the theft originates from outside "customers"; much may also be attributable to inside staff.

The costs of theft and shrinkage to an organization can lead to a substantial drain on available cash. Thus a 2% shrinkage rate on annual sales of $1 million, represents a cash loss of $20,000 - certainly enough to pay for a winter holiday to Bermuda several times over!

Indeed, theft and embezzlement can spell disaster for a small company. According to an American study about 30% of all business failures are attributable to these causes. This should be a very sobering thought for the start-up entrepreneur!

The first step in controlling shrinkage is to find out what goes missing and how much of it. The only way to do this is through good inventory control with actual counts.

The next step is to institute measures to combat the problem.

In a retail establishment such measures could vary from rearranging the layout of the store, to eliminating hidden corners. Consideration should be given to removing high displays and store fixtures and replacing them with lower ones (maximum of 54" in height is common) so that everybody in the store can be seen.

Hidden or visible surveillance cameras can be introduced. Electronic tags could be attached to merchandise. More security floorwalkers could be employed and two-way mirrors installed. All these measures can be very cost effective in reducing shrinkage and theft.

Employee theft can be very subtle. Examples might be notepaper that goes missing; personal letters that go out mixed up with the corporate mail and that beast of a photocopy machine. Unnecessary photocopying costs U.S. industry $2.6 billion annually! [C.B.C. Radio: *As It Happens*, August 25, 1986]. This is easy to control - lock the machine up so only certain people have access to it and make sure that every copy is accounted for.

Rental Space Costs

Rental of space is one of the major costs facing small business. Examination of the use of space may reveal areas for effective cost cutting.

Is the space being used efficiently?

If a business is seasonal or cyclical - would the temporary use of outside warehousing space be more economical during peak periods?

Is space being used to store dead files; old inventory or plain "junk"? Could a switch to microfilm for storing records eliminate a lot of office space?

Is the company paying a premium for prestige space that is not really necessary? Prestige is a game for banks - they can afford it (with your money!). Is it better to have low cost rental space and some profits or high cost rental space and no profits?

Question whether much of your space is necessary in the first place.

Subcontracted work can reduce space requirements. Many salespeople can work at home from a telephone. Much of the work that a bookkeeper does can be done at home.

The computer terminal makes working at home a new reality. Providing controls are in place to ensure that work is actually performed; having certain employees work at home could provide significant savings on rental space costs.

If there is excess space - can it be sublet and provide additional income? Can you share space with somebody else to reduce costs?

Many business centres provide small unit rentals, together with communal telephone answering, secretarial and other services - including the use of boardrooms and other facilities on a fee-for-use basis.

Working Out of Your Home or Apartment

Start-up overheads can certainly be reduced by working out of your home or apartment. Just be careful how you do it!

Most residential leases prohibit the use of premises for business purposes, however, many landlords will turn a blind eye so long as the rent is paid on time and you don't disturb the neighbours. If it is a high traffic business, such as retail, where there are people constantly coming and going, there is likely to be trouble, especially when the neighbours start to complain.

Also, watch those municipal bylaws and zoning regulations! These are designed to restrict business to regulated areas and prohibit it in others. So if you're not in an area zoned for business, you are theoretically breaking the law. Again, if you don't flaunt it with lawn signs and lots of people coming and going, the chances are that nobody will notice.

If you intend to work out of your home, you are not alone! The National Home Business Institute has estimated that 3.6 million Canadians work out of their homes. This represents about 30% of Canada's labourforce. This percentage is similar to an estimate put out by the Federal Business Development Bank [now called the Business Development Bank].

Don't forget that there are some tax advantages if you use part of your residence as your principal place of business! You can use the rent relating to that business area as a legitimate business expense.

17

EXPANDING

Entering the Expansion Mode

If your business is involved in producing a product, it is usual for companies to establish themselves in their local market first, before taking on more distant areas. This process would normally continue until the company is represented nationally. After this, there comes a question of taking on foreign markets.

Marketing overseas presents a challenge for most North American companies since, language and cultures are different in foreign lands. In addition, the entrepreneur is faced with different regulations, redesigning of packaging, translation of advertising and promotional materials together with a great deal of travel to establish local agents or distributors. Not only that, as exporter, the entrepreneur faces many new challenges, such as, making sure that payment is received for goods delivered.

Once the business has reached this stage, debt financing is generally a lot easier to obtain since the company has built up assets and has developed a track record of its own. In addition to that, it can now be taken seriously by government departments and agencies, many of which have a mandate to assist exporters, since this leads to job creation back home.

For other companies that are not involved in producing products, there are other ways in which to expand and we will consider some of these in the following text.

Can You Franchise Your Business Concept?

Franchising is a complex business. It requires a great deal of skill, effort and time in order to establish a successful operation.

In determining whether your business would be a suitable candidate for franchising, you must obviously have advanced beyond the prototype stage. The finished product or service must be out there on the market and have more than just a few months of operation under its belt.

It should have some kind of a track record to show that there is truly a market demand for it. As a further extension to this thought, the business must be profitable. Nobody in his right mind is going to buy a franchise of a money losing operation.

Ideally, the franchisor should have several company owned outlets in operation before offering franchisees an opportunity to participate. This allows the kinks to be worked out and the operation procedures to be put into place.

Then, there is the expense of developing the franchise program itself, including the preparation of all the legal and accounting documentation that will be required for your franchise contracts. This is an up-front expense and it is important to do it right the first time.

It won't be difficult to burn through $100,000 or a great deal more in developing such a program. The cost will obviously be a function of the type of franchise and how much is involved in establishing it.

Having said all this, the rewards can be great. Look around you! There are franchise operations galore.

Most franchisees are successful because they are following a proven success formula and the franchisor gets to benefit from all their efforts. Franchising certainly offers a formula for fast-track method of financing growth by using other peoples' capital and energy.

Could Licensing be the Answer?

One way out of the morass of strategic planning, business plans, late nights and financial heartburn is to hand the whole thing over to somebody else. This can certainly be done with products that are unique and especially those that are protected by a patent.

Happiness is the licensing of a product to some hard working fellow, who does all the work to produce it and sell it and who will also pay you a royalty for the privilege of doing so - which in turn will allow you to laze all day in the sun on the beach!

The key to successful licensing arrangements is protection of the product or process by a patent (or a "secret" formula as in the case of some soft drink companies).

Once you have obtained the legal rights to the design or the process; you are in a strong position to license the use of your patent. Licensing can be done on an international basis and the selling of rights abroad can lead to significant possibilities for income generation.

In addition to marketing licensing rights yourself, there are a number of companies which will purchase royalty rights from inventors with a view to commercializing the product themselves or in conjunction with others.

Licensing can also be used in joint venture agreements. An example might be a company that has developed a new technology but does not have the resources to produce it or market it. Such a company might be able to enter into a joint venture agreement with a company that has the required resources.

Another form of licensing is to have an outside company manufacture the product for you whilst you take charge of the marketing effort yourself.

Of course, licensing can be a powerful way of expanding your market reach beyond your local area. Thus, you could licence your product for sale in foreign markets. Such arrangements could permit modification of the product to meet local conditions or preferences.

17

THE POT OF GOLD

Going Public - the End of a Long Journey?

Going public may be the ultimate dream of many small business owners. Here is a pot of gold at the end of the rainbow that is a reward for all their labours. They can now buy their dream houses and dream yachts!

"Going Public" means selling part of the ownership of a company in the form of shares to the public. This is usually done through the facilities of one of the stock exchanges.

There are two considerations to make in the decision to go public. Is the objective to finance the company or is it for the owners to cash in on their investment? In many instances, it is a combination of both.

For the diehard entrepreneur who wants to cash out, going public provides the money to start another company and do it all over again!

On the other hand, the small business owner may want to keep as much of the company as possible and simply use the funds for expansion so that the pot of gold will be bigger on the day the chips are finally cashed in. This is usually the case with smaller companies.

Going public also provides an "out" for the venture capitalist. It enables him to cash in on his investment (if he so desires) and put his money into other deals.

There are however, rules to regulate the sale of the original owners' stock.

Escrow provisions require that the owners hold their stock in trust until permission is obtained for their release. This is usually granted after certain conditions have been met. The procedure is designed to prevent the original owners from vanishing overnight and to provide some continuity in the fortunes of the company.

The sale of shares to the public in the United States is governed by the Securities and Exchange Commission. In Canada it is governed by the various provincial securities commissions. These are designed to protect the public from abuses but can also be quite onerous on the entrepreneur who wishes to raise equity capital.

How Big Do You Have to Be to Go Public?

Access to public markets is usually far easier for medium and larger sized businesses than for small business. Thus, companies with sales in excess of $5 million per year and a good growth record should find fairly ready acceptance in the marketplace.

Smaller companies can certainly attempt to go public; but whether their shares will be bought by the public is another matter. A number of exchanges in the United States and Canada will allow small companies to list or "trade over the counter" on an unlisted market.

The first time a company offers shares to the public, it is called an "Initial Public Offering" or "IPO".

Going public is an expensive and time consuming process. Listing on a major exchange could incur costs well in excess of $100,000 although one could possibly get away with $50,000 for a small listing on one of the smaller exchanges, such as Vancouver or Alberta.

Obviously, going public is not something that can be done easily by the very small business. The chances of success increase with size, combined with bright prospects for future growth. As I said at the beginning of this chapter, going public is a great way for founding entrepreneurs to cash in their chips and pick up their pot of gold at the end of the rainbow.

18

CONCLUSION

Keep on Learning

This book will have provided you with the essential basics for starting your own successful business. Hopefully, it has been thought-provoking and has given you some insight into some of the things that you have to consider before venturing out on your own.

Unfortunately, a short book such as this cannot cover everything and I would strongly recommend that you seek out advice and books relating to your new endeavour. Indeed, I would also recommend that you continue to read and attend seminars on various topics on entrepreneurship. Many people have travelled the same path before and you can benefit from their experience and mistakes.

In addition, technology presents all of us with the new challenges, since it will alter many traditional ways of doing business. In so doing, it will create a multitude of opportunities and it is up to **you**, as a new entrepreneur, to seize the initiative and take advantage of everything that new technology has to offer. In order to do this, you must be prepared to spend a lot of time reading newspapers, magazines and books, in addition to attending seminars and talks, so as to keep up with the rapidly changing world of business. If you fail to do this, you may be left behind trying to feed dinosaurs, when in fact there are none to feed!

In addition, as a business owner, you will need to acquire a number of skills if you do not already have them. For example, you will probably have to learn how to make presentations and how to speak in public. In this connection, I could recommend an excellent book (which we happen to publish) called: "Speak with Confidence Now".

If you are an inventor, you will probably wanted to protect your invention. In this regard you may be interested in three other books which we publish. The first is: *Can you make Money with Your Idea or Invention?* by business consultant Don Lunny. The next two deal with protecting your ideas and are as follows: *Protect Your Intellectual Property: An International Guide to Patents, Copyrights, and Trademarks* written by two experts in this area and another one targeted towards in the Canadian inventor called: *The Canadian Business Guide to Patents for Inventions and New Products* by patent attorney, George Rolston.

The books mentioned above are published by Productive Publications and are written by different authors. In addition, I have written to books which should assist you. The first is: *Marketing for Beginners-how to Get Your Products Into the Hands of Consumers* and the second is: *Software for Small Business-a Review of the Latest Programs to Help You Improve Business Efficiency and Productivity;* which will be published and updated every year and cover software that works on the PC platform.

Running your own business takes a great deal of time and effort, and you will find that you need to sacrifice a lot along the way. Inevitably, you will make some mistakes but the most important thing is to learn from them and try to avoid repeating them again in the future. In addition, you should try to read as much as you can and attend as many seminars as your time permits; both on business procedures and on new technology, so that you can stay ahead of the curve.

In closing, I should tell you that I have been running my own businesses for over 20 years and looking back, I wish I had done a few things differently, however, I never regretted having gone out of my own. I welcome you to the club!

Good luck!

BOOKS TO HELP YOU SUCCEED

✓ How to Start a Business ✓

✓ Where to Get Financing ✓

✓ Marketing & Exporting ✓

✓ Software for Business ✓

✓ Computer Security ✓

✓ Books about the Internet ✓

✓ Tax Havens & Investing ✓

✓ Get a Great Job ✓

PRODUCTIVE PUBLICATIONS
Our 14th Year Helping Readers
With the New Economy

Start Your Own Business: Be Your Own Boss!

Your Road Map to Independence

By: Iain Williamson

Learn from someone who has done it!

There really is a pot of gold at the end of the rainbow if you've got what it takes! Find out where to get ideas for a business and how to check them out. Why location is so important. How to research the market. How to plan for success. How to calculate how much money you will really need and where to get it. Growing pains and managing employees...plus lots of other things you will need to know.

Iain Williamson has run his own businesses for over 20 years and has also acted as a consultant to many small business owners. He shares his experiences with you in this book. Use it as YOUR Road Map to Independence!

Start Your Own Business - Be Your Own Boss: Your Road Map to Independence By Iain Williamson: 208 pages; Softcover, ISBN 1-896210-96-1: $29.95 plus $5.00 postage & handling plus GST. Order Your Copy Now

Becoming Successful!

Taking your home-based business to a new level

By: Don Varner

Strategies For Getting Great Results In Your Home-Based Business!

How to turn any type of business into a SUCCESSFUL Business! Everything You Need To Know - Made Easy!

- Self-Improvement
- Handling Rejections
- Management Skills
- 16 Ways to Prospect
- Designing Great Ads
- and much, much more!
- Self-Motivation
- Hiring Tips
- Motivating Employees
- Closing Sales
- No-Cost Ways to Advertise

Becoming Successful! Taking your home-based business to a new level by: Don Varner; 338 pages; ISBN 1-896210-87-2; Softcover: $39.95 + $5.00 postage & handling + GST. Order Now

MAKE IT ON YOUR OWN!

How to Succeed in Your Own Business

By: Barrie Jackson

What it takes to run a business and make it succeed Contains practical, hands-on information, for immediate use. Learn from the author's personal experience and mistakes. Lots of anecdotes from the author's business adventures which make for interesting reading with a "practical punch"

Before his untimely death, **BARRIE JACKSON**, forged Cooper Boating Centre into Canada's largest yacht charter company.

MAKE IT ON YOUR OWN! How to Succeed in Your Own Business: by Barrie Jackson, 212 pages, ISBN 1-896210-37-6; softcover, $29.95 + $5.00 postage + GST.

Your Guide to Starting & Self-Financing Your Own Business in Canada

Revised 1998-99 Edition

By: Iain Williamson

Learn to start and bootstrap your own business. Have you got what it takes? How much capital do you really need? Learn to establish a marketing strategy. Where you can get the latest marketing information. Chapter on how computers can help your small business. Can you self-finance the business yourself?

Your Guide to Starting & Self-Financing Your Own Business in Canada: 1998-99 Edition; by Iain Williamson; 200 pages; Softcover; ISBN 1-896210-67-8; ISSN 1191-0518: $24.95 plus $5.00 postage & handling plus GST

Your Guide to Preparing a Plan to Raise Money for Your Own Business

Revised 1998-99 Edition

By: Iain Williamson

A good business plan is essential to succeed in your quest for financing. Contains a step-by-step guide to create your own winning plan. Computer software you can use. Learn how to address the concerns of investors or lenders. Tips on structuring your plan. Contains a sample plan to show you an example

The author is a consultant with many years of experience in preparing plans for business clients.

Your Guide to Preparing a Plan to Raise Money for Your Own Business: 1998-99 Edition by Iain Williamson, 158 pages, softcover, ISBN 1-896210-68-6; ISSN 1191-0496: $24.95 plus $5.00 postage & handling plus GST.

12 Separate Editions - One for Each Province & Territory

In spite of cutbacks, lots of assistance is still available to you

Your Guide to Government Financial Assistance for Business

Your Guide to Government Financial Assistance for Business

1998-99 Edition

IAIN WILLIAMSON

Completely Revised and Updated for 1998-99

Business financing in Canada is in a constant state of flux. New government programs are continually being introduced. Old ones are often amended or discontinued with little publicity. These books will help you:

*   Obtain the most up-to-date details of every government business assistance program in your province or territory;

*   Get the right phone numbers & addresses to save your time and put you in contact with the program managers;

*   Learn about the effectiveness of many federal programs;

*   Find out what programs will help your business and how to apply.

These books are all you need to obtain the latest information, since they have been recently revised.

Covers all federal and provincial or territorial programs in your area

There are hundreds of programs to help your business. Take advantage of them!

There are literally hundreds of programs and sub-programs to help your business grow. It's up to you to find out what is available and how to access them! These books will help you and let you decide which ones are best suited to your business.

Your Guide to Government Financial Assistance for Business in

EDITION	ISBN	ISSN	PAGES
Newfoundland and Labrador	1896210732	1198-0508	27
Prince Edward Island	1896210740	1198-0532	25
Nova Scotia	1896210759	1198-0516	30
New Brunswick	1896210767	1198-0494	26
Quebec	1896210775	1198-0540	32
Ontario	1896210783	1198-0524	33
Manitoba	1896210791	1198-0486	32
Saskatchewan	1896210805	1198-0559	31
Alberta	1896210813	1198-046X	31
British Columbia	1896210821	1198-0478	318
The Yukon	1896210848	1198-0575	232
The Northwest Territories	189621083X	1198-0567	24

Softcover: each cost $39.95 + $5.00 postage/handling + GST. Order your copy now on the Order Form on pages 19-20.

Written by an Acknowledged Authority

Iain Williamson, of Entrepreneurial Business Consultants of Canada, has over 29 years experience as a financial analyst in the stockbrokerage business and as owner-manager of his own companies. Now a consultant, author and seminar leader, his clients have included a national accounting firm, private companies and business organizations. He holds degrees from St. Andrew's University and from Oxford. His reviews can help you evaluate the effectiveness of many programs.

Get the Latest Details for Your Province or Territory Order Your Copy NOW!

Your Guide to Raising Venture Capital for Your Own Business in Canada

Revised and Updated 1998-99 Edition

By: Iain Williamson

Formal and informal venture capitalists provide risk capital. Find out who they are; what they offer and how to find them. Updated chapters on Labour Sponsored Venture Capital. Corporations and on Government Funds. Find out what they are looking for, how they evaluate deals and how to negotiate with them. The author is a business consultant who has successfully raised venture capital.

Your Guide to Raising Venture Capital for Your Own Business in Canada: 1998-99 Edition; by Iain Williamson: 226 pages; Softcover; ISBN 1-896210-69-4; ISSN 1191-0534: $29.95 plus $5.00 postage & handling plus GST.

Your Guide to Arranging Bank & Debt Financing for Your Own Business in Canada

Revised and Updated 1998-99 Edition

By: Iain Williamson

Learn the secrets of successful debt financing in Canada. Find out who the players are in Canadian banking. Do you qualify for the new high risk, unsecured loans? How to prepare your company before you approach lenders. Find out how your loan application is evaluated. Can factoring or leasing help you? The author has many years of experience in bank financing and leasing.

Your Guide to Arranging Bank & Debt Financing for Your Own Business in Canada: 1998-99 Edition; by Iain Williamson; 178 pages; Softcover; ISBN 1-896210-70-8; ISSN 1191-0542: $26.95 + $5.00 postage & handling + GST.

Your Guide to Financing Business Growth by Selling a Piece of the Pie

What's involved in going public; employee share ownership plans and franchising in Canada

Revised and Updated 1998-99 Edition

By: Iain Williamson

A critical examination of three methods of growing your business by using other people's money. How to sell shares to the public or to your employees. How to expand through franchising. The author was a financial analyst in the Canadian stockbrokerage business.

Your Guide to Financing Business Growth by Selling a Piece of the Pie: what's involved in going public; employee share ownership plans and franchising in Canada: 1998-99 Edition; by Iain Williamson; 102 pages; Softcover; ISBN 1-896210-71-6; ISSN 1191-0488: $18.95 plus $5.00 postage plus GST. Order your copy now by completing the Order Form

Your Guide to Canadian Export Financing

Successful Techniques for Financing Your Exports from Canada

Revised 1998-99 Edition

By: Iain Williamson

Practical techniques for financing exports. Get details of all provincial and federal assistance programs that help you export including addresses and phone numbers to steer you in the right direction. The author is a consultant and entrepreneur who knows the practical side of importing and exporting.

Your Guide to Canadian Export Financing: 1998-99 Edition; by Iain Williamson; 148 pages; softcover; ISBN 1-896210-72-4; $26.95 + $5.00 postage/handling + GST. Order your copy NOW.

Market Overseas with Canadian Government Help

By: Don Lunny

Finding Overseas Buyers
Meeting New Customers
Displaying Products Abroad
Conducting Market Research
Government Assistance
Export and Import Permits
Reading to Find Markets
Other helpful sources

Export Questionnaire
Distributors Questionnaire
Export Costing/Pricing
Goods and Services Tax
Thinking in Global Terms
Start with North America
The Bank and the Exporter
Private Sector Financing

Market Overseas with Canadian Government Help by Don Lunny, 68 pages; ISBN 0-920847-87-0; softcover: $19.95 + $5.00 post/handling + GST.

Reach the Global Marketplace

A Canadian Guide to Researching Foreign Markets and Online Sources

By: Richard B. McEachin

Advice on hiring an outside researcher. Shows you what is available online and in print. Written for both the newcomer and the experienced exporter. Author, **Richard B. McEachin,** is an expert with over 20 years experience in gathering and analyzing intelligence material.

Reach the Global Marketplace - A Canadian Guide to Researching Foreign Markets and Online Sources by Richard B. McEachin, 193 pages; ISBN 0-920847-92-7; softcover: $24.95 + $5.00 post/handling + GST. Order yours now

Your Homebased Business Plan -Also- Working With Your Banker

By: Donald Lunny

SECTION I - The Business Plan for Homebased Business: a step-by-step guide to writing your plan.

SECTION II - Working with your Banker: the fundamentals of borrowing and how they affect you.

Donald Lunny: an entrepreneur and consultant with many years experience in organizing and restructuring companies.

Your Homebased Business Plan -Also- Working With Your Banker by Donald Lunny: 52 p; softcover; ISBN 0-920847-35-8: $14.95 + $5.00 postage/handling + GST. Order your copy now!

Shoplifting, Security, Curtailing Crime - Inside & Out

by Don Lunny

If you are a shopkeeper or business owner, this practical, hands-on book will alert you to the alarming theft rates you may be exposed to. From petty theft, bad cheques to armed robbery, you get advice on dealing with the situation and how to train staff.

Discusses internal theft by employees - how you can recognize it and how to reduce it. If it alerts you to just one problem, it could pay for itself many, many times over.

Shoplifting, Security, Curtailing Crime - Inside & Out: by Don Lunny; 115 pages; softcover; ISBN 0-920847-66-8: $29.95 + $5.00 postage/handling + GST.

MEETING THE SAMURAI

Two Hundred Power Strategies for Doing Business in Japan

By: Jonathan King

Author, **Jonathan King**, learned the language and worked in Japan for six years as a business consultant and director to two Japanese "Fortune 500" companies. In this book he shows you how to export your products to the heart of Asia's largest, yet toughest economic market.

MEETING THE SAMURAI: Two Hundred Power Strategies for Doing Business in Japan: by Jonathan King, 119 pages, softcover, ISBN 1-896210-40-6; $19.95 plus $5.00 postage & handling plus GST. Order your copy now

Tips for Entrepreneurs

How to meet the challenges of starting and managing your own business

Henry Kyambalesa

This book is the culmination of a 3-year research study into the challenges faced by entrepreneurs when they become their own boss. Tips for those about to start a business & tips for those already in business. Decide whether self-employment is for you. Practical advice on getting started. The skills you will need

Tips for Entrepreneurs: How to meet the challenges of starting and managing your own business: by Henry Kyambalesa: 194 pages, softcover; ISBN 1-896210-85-6; $26.95 + $5.00 postage/handling + GST.

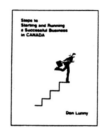

Steps to Starting and Running a Successful Business in CANADA

by Don Lunny

Managing your own business can be a rewarding experience but survival can be tough in today's economy. This book shows you the essential steps to ensure that your business is profitable.

Steps to Starting and Running a Successful Business in CANADA by Don Lunny, 190 pages; ISBN 0-920847-85-4; softcover: $34.95 + $5.00 post/handling + GST. Order your copy now.

Checklist for Going into Business

By: Don Lunny

Points to create your own profitable business if this is your dream. Starting it is reality. But, there is a gap between your dream and reality - that can only be filled with careful planning. You need a plan to avoid pitfalls, to achieve your goals and make profits. This guide helps you prepare a comprehensive business plan and determine if your idea is feasible.

DON LUNNY is an experienced business owner and consultant with many years of experience.

Checklist for Going into Business by Don Lunny, 53 pages; ISBN 0-920847-86-2; softcover: $19.95 + $5.00 post/handling + GST. Order your copy now

Marketing for Beginners

How to Get Your Products into the Hands of Consumers

By: Iain Williamson

Covers the basics of marketing for new entrepreneurs. How to make people aware of your products. How to get them to buy. How to get products into the hands of consumers. Traditional channels of distribution versus direct marketing. One-on-one marketing versus mass marketing. A look at the Internet as a marketing tool.

Ways to promote and advertise your products. After-sales service and the lifetime value of your customers. Sources of marketing information. The author has been marketing products for 20 years.

Marketing for Beginners: How to Get Your Products into the Hands of Consumers: by Iain Williamson: 215 pages, softcover; ISBN 1-896210-97-X; $29.95 + $5.00 postage/handling + GST.

Marketing Beyond 2000

Why you will have to use the Internet to market your goods or services in the 21st. Century

by Iain Williamson

The Internet will become an awesome marketing tool in the 21st. Century. Learn how its current limitations are being overcome. Take a look at the future of radio, TV and newspapers Glimpse at the marketplace of the future. The author says it's up to you to take advantage of this tremendous marketing tool. Find out how!

Marketing Beyond 2000: Why you will have to use the Internet to market your goods or services in the 21st. Century by Iain Williamson, 194 pages, ISBN 1-896210-66-X; softcover; $27.95 + $5.00 postage/handling + GST.

Successful Direct Mail Marketing in Canada

A Step-by-Step Guide to Selling Your Products or Services Through the Mail

by Iain Williamson

Techniques to Make Money in the Highly Competitive Direct Mail Market. Direct mail as an inexpensive way to reach customers. Ways to keep your costs to a minimum. How to save on postage by using bulk rates. How to get the most out of your computer.

The author has over 14 years experience in selling by direct mail.

Successful Direct Mail Marketing in Canada: A Step-by-Step Guide to Selling Your Products or Services Through the Mail: Iain Williamson: 114 pg, softcover; ISBN 1-896210-39-2; $19.95 + $5.00 postage/handling + GST. Order Your Copy Now.

The Basics for Sales Success

An essential guide for new sales representatives, entrepreneurs and business people

By Bill Sobye

An introductory book which covers the basic points on how to:

- Find customers
- Dress for success
- Set goals
- Success and rejection
- Study your prospects
- Handle "the butterflies"
- How to include humour
- Business versus pleasure

Bill Sobye has 28 years of experience as a Sales Manager.

The Basics for Sales Success by Bill Sobye: 157 pages; Softcover; ISBN 1-896210-65-1: $24.95 plus $5.00 postage & handling plus GST. Order Your Copy Now!

Selling by Mail Order and Independence

by Donald Lunny

Your step-by-step guide to seeking independence with your own mail order business. Also invaluable, if you are an established business owner who wants to add a mail order department or to purchase an existing mail order business. Learn the essentials from **Donald Lunny** who is a business consultant with over 25 years experience in sales, marketing and promotion in Canada.

Selling by Mail Order and Independence by Donald Lunny: 109 pages; Softcover; ISBN 0-920847-24-2: $16.95 plus $5.00 postage/handling plus GST. Order your copy now

Evaluating Franchise Opportunities

by Don Lunny

Although the success rate for franchisee-owned businesses is better than for many other start-up businesses, success is not guaranteed. Don't be "pressured" into a franchise that is not right for you. Investigate your options. Find out how to evaluate the business, the franchisor, the franchise package, and yourself.

Author and business consultant, **Don Lunny**, shows you how to avoid the pitfalls <u>before</u> you make a franchise investment.

Evaluating Franchise Opportunities by Don Lunny; 75 pages; softcover; ISBN 0-920847-64-1: $19.95 + $5.00 P/H + GST

Cooperative Time Management

Get more done and have more fun!

Chance Massaro & Katheryn Allen-Katz

Learn how to define appropriate and important work; how to plan, schedule and defend "quality" work time and how to work effectively with other employees.

Cooperative Time Management: Get more done and have more fun! by Chance Massaro & Katheryn Allen-Katz 224 pages, softcover; ISBN 1-896210-86-4; $34.95 + $5.00 postage/handling + GST.

THE LEAN OFFICE

How to Use Just-in-Time Techniques to Streamline Your Office

By: Jim Thompson

This book is for everyone who works in an office. Find out how to foster and nurture employee involvement and put excitement back into continuous improvement. Get the tools needed to improve office productivity. Most importantly, reduce employee stress and frustration, while improving productivity. Find out how this happens <u>with</u> employees, not <u>to</u> employees!

Jim Thompson is a lean production consultant who studied these systems first-hand while with GM and Toyota in California.

The Lean Office - How to Use Just-in-Time Techniques to Streamline Your Office: by Jim Thompson, 138 pg, softcover, ISBN 1-896210-41-4; $24.95 + $5.00 post + GST. Order now!

LEAN PRODUCTION

How to Use the Highly Effective Japanese Concept of Kaizen to Improve Your Efficiency

By: Jim Thompson

Learn specific techniques and behaviours to improve your effectiveness. Find out about a system that has been used very effectively at the organizational level for over forty years.

Author, **Jim Thompson** has held senior management positions with General Motors and the Walker Manufacturing Company. Now a consultant, he popularizes lean production techniques to eliminate waste and restore sanity to our lives.

LEAN PRODUCTION - How to Use the Highly Effective Japanese Concept of Kaizen to Improve Your Efficiency by Jim Thompson, 146 pages, softcover, ISBN 1-896210-42-2; $24.95 + $5.00 postage + GST. Order now

Protect Your Intellectual Property

An International Guide to Patents, Copyrights and Trademarks

By: Hoyt L. Barber & Robert M. Logan

An abundance of information on step-by-step procedures to obtain exclusive protection for unique ideas, inventions, name identifying marks, or artistic, literary, musical, photographic o cinematographic works.

Protect Your Intellectual Property: An International Guide t Patents, Copyrights and Trademarks by Hoyt L. Barber Robert M. Logan, 305 pages, softcover, ISBN 1-896210-95-3 $59 .95 plus $5.00 postage & handling plus GST. Order your cop now

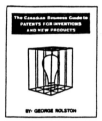

The Canadian Busines Guide to Patents fo Inventions an New Product

By: George Rolston

This is your complete reference to patenting around the world. Th key elements in the patent process. When to search for earlie patents. When you should file patent applications. The importance of your patent filing date. Understand the critical wording of paten claims. Getting the best out of your patent agent. What the paten office will do for you. What to do if your patent application i rejected. How to go about patenting in foreign countries and how to negotiate a licence agreement. **George Rolston**, is a barriste and solicitor who has specialized in patents for over 30 years.

The Canadian Business Guide to Patents for Inventions and New Products by George Rolston: 202 pg; ISBN 0-920847-13-7 Softcover: $48.00 + $5.00 P/H + GST.

Can You Make Money with Your Idea or Invention?

By: Don Lunny

- Can you Exploit it?
- How to produce it
- Can you make money?
- Where to get help
- Industrial Design
- Copyright
- Points of caution
- Patent applications
- Sample licensing agreement

- Is the idea original?
- How to distribute it
- Can you protect it?
- A word about patents
- Trademarks
- First steps
- Possible problems
- What are your chances?

Can You Make Money with Your Idea or Invention? by Don Lunny; 99 pages; softcover; ISBN 0-920847-65-X; $24.95 + $5.00 postage/handling + GST.

Software for Small Business

1999 Edition

A review of the latest programs to help you improve business efficiency and productivity using Windows 95 and Windows 98

By: Iain Williamson

For new and experienced users. Covers operating systems, word processing, desktop publishing, voice dictation, graphics, video, photos, spreadsheets, accounting, databases, contact management, communications, Internet software, security and virus protection.

Software for Small Business: 1999 Edition: A Review of the Latest Programs to Help You Improve Business Efficiency and Productivity Using Windows 95 and Windows 98 by Iain Williamson: 235 pages, softcover; ISBN 1-896210-88-0; $29.95 + $5.00 postage/handling + GST.

Are You Ready for Information Warfare?

Security for Personal Computers, Networks and Telecommunication Systems

by Gregory J. Petrakis, Ph.D.

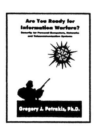

This book is an antidote against hackers and information theft. Access to data is so easy to obtain and it can be stolen or modified. Informational infrastructures can also be destroyed. This book shows you how to counter-attack.

The author is an expert in this field and is Adjunct Professor at the University of Missouri-Kansas City.

Are You Ready for Information Warfare? Security for Personal Computers, Networks and Telecommunication Systems by Gregory J. Petrakis, Ph.D., 206 pages, softcover; ISBN 1-896210-94-5; $34.95 + $5.00 postage/handling + GST.

THE ONLINE WORLD

How to Profit from the Information Superhighway

By: Mike Weaver and Odd de Presno

This book will change the way you learn, find a job, get information & do business. By the year 2000, the Internet will have one billion users. Can you afford to ignore this market?

Odd de Presno, from Norway, is a consultant and **Mike Weaver**, from Saskatchewan, is winner of the Saskatchewan Association for Computers in Education/Apple Teacher Award of Excellence.

THE ONLINE WORLD: How to Profit from the Information Superhighway: by Mike Weaver and Odd de Presno: 302 pages, softcover; ISBN 0-920847-89-7; $39.95 + $5.00 P/H + GST.

She Delivers Steel

Inspiration from a Grandmother who Drove Her Dream to Reality

By: Patricia Prior

Fulfill your dreams - accomplish your goals both physical and emotional! At age 43, Patricia Prior left a successful career in motivational speaking to fulfill her dream of becoming a truck driver. She hauled steel through the Rockies to Vancouver and seven years later she became a grandmother! Her story reflects the true concept of real accomplishment. The journey is rewarding. Read this book and enjoy the trip!

She Delivers Steel: Inspiration from a Grandmother who Drove Her Dream to Reality: by Patricia Prior: 162 pages, softcover; ISBN 1-896210-92-9; $24.95 + $5.00 Postage + GST.

Speak with Confidence NOW!

A Simple, Unique Program Designed to Make You a Confident, Effective, Dynamic Speaker Every Day, in Every Situation!

By Steve Ryan

Surveys show that speaking in public is our greatest fear. Top-rated radio host and training expert, Steve Ryan, shows you how to make presentations using dynamic speech. Conquer nervousness, improve your breathing habits and enunciation. Learn to avoid vocal mistakes. How to project yourself and use vocabulary and body language advantageously.

Author, **Steve Ryan** hosts the top-rated *KILO/Colorado Springs Morning Show*. He has over 16 years experience in radio.

Speak with Confidence NOW! By Steve Ryan: 168 pages; Softcover; ISBN 1-896210-62-7: $24.95 plus $5.00 postage & handling plus GST.

Let's be Reasonable!

Effective ways to handle difficult people

By: Clive Lilwall

This book will help you deal with the difficult people in your business and personal lives. It discusses numerous reasons for nastiness and offers you many practical solutions.

Clive Lilwall has taught human communications and writing at Durham College for 28 years and shows you effective ways to handle the difficult people in your life.

Let's be Reasonable! Effective ways to handle difficult people by: Clive Lilwall; 172 pages; Softcover; ISBN 1-896210-64-3: $29.95 + $5.00 postage & handling + GST. Order Now.

The Internet Job Search Guide

By Cathy & Dan Noble

A thorough and comprehensive guide to finding employment opportunities using the Internet. You will learn about resume assistance; career guidance; research and networking. This book takes a step-by-step approach. Contains hundreds of Internet addresses covering a wide spectrum of employment opportunities. This guide will help both first-time users as well as experienced net surfers. It is concise and easy to read.

The Internet Job Search Guide By Cathy & Dan Noble: 208 pages; Softcover; ISBN 1-896210-63-5: $29.95 plus $5.00 postage & handling plus GST. Order Your Copy Now!

How to Get a Really Great Job!

A complete program if you hate your job and don't know how to go about changing it

by Donald L Varner

This book is written for people at any age; at any educational level; for any field; in any market! If you follow Don Varner's advice, you can watch your happiness and your salary soar... as your job turns into a career!

How to Get a Really Great Job! A complete program if you hate your job and don't know how to go about changing it by Donald L. Varner, 240 pages; Softcover; ISBN 1-896210-90-2: $29.95 plus $5.00 postage/handling plus GST. Order your copy now

30 Minutes to a Better Job!

Step-by-step instructions for getting a better job made easy!

by Don Varner

This book applies to any age, any educational level and in any field! It shows you how to get a job that makes you happy! Earn more money! Create killer résumés! Free job counselling! Secrets of interviewing! Make them want you! How to land that great job! Locate over 33,000 jobs & their salaries!

"The only job security in today's society is knowing where the next job is and how to get it!"

30 Minutes to a Better Job! Step-by-step instructions for getting a better job made easy! Don Varner; 52 pg; ISBN 1-896210-89-9 softcover;: $9.95 + $5.00 P/H + GST

HOW TO SELL YOURSELF INTO A JOB

Successful Job Hunting Using Sales and Marketing Know-how

By: Dr. Ray Mesluk

Worried about the difficult questions you might be asked in an interview? Are you focussed on your lack of experience? Do you like to talk about your accomplishments and qualifications? Stop thinking "my failings", "my successes". Stop thinking "me".

Learn from **Dr. Ray Mesluk**, an expert with a Ph.D. in Mathematics who has applied sales and marketing techniques in his job searches. He has worked for a leading recruitment firm.

HOW TO SELL YOURSELF INTO A JOB - Successful Job Hunting Using Sales and Marketing Know-how by Dr. Ray Mesluk, 184 pages; ISBN 0-920847-91-9; softcover: $29.95 + $5.00 postage/handling + GST.

SUCCESS is the Best Revenge: Gold Medal Career Management

By: John Stewardson and Bob Evans

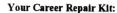
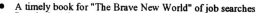

Your Career Repair Kit:

- A timely book for "The Brave New World" of job searches
- Practical advice to show you how to win at the career game
- Read it if you are employed or are looking for a job

John Stewardson and **Bob Evans**, between them have fifty years experience in human resources, contract operating executives and executive outplacement and career planning.

SUCCESS is the Best Revenge: Gold Medal Career Management: by John Stewardson and Bob Evans; 277 pages, softcover, ISBN 0-920847-88-9; $39.95 + $5.00 P/H + GST.

HOW TO GET A JOB!

By: Paul Shearstone

Learn interview fundamentals	How to prepare mentally
What makes a good resume	Distinguish types of interviewers
Ways to maintain credibility	Reason for different questions
Master the confident answer	How to turn the tables
How to ask for the job	How to GET THE JOB!

Paul Shearstone is President of Colby Lewis Management Consultants and an experienced recruiter and sales trainer.

How to Get a Job! by Paul Shearstone; softcover:
English Edition: 54 pages; ISBN 0-920847-36-6: $14.95.
French\English Bilingual Edition: ISBN 0-920847-37-4: $24.95

STOCK MARKET PANIC!

How to Prosper
in the Coming Bear Market

Dave Skarica

A warning of the times ahead that every mutual fund or stock investor should read. Sober thoughts on what may happen and how to profit from it! The sharp sell-off in late August 1998 was just a warning! It showed us how confidence can be eroded overnight. How do you avoid watching your wealth evaporate? Find out what to avoid and How to Prosper in the Coming Crash!

Stock Market Panic! How to Prosper in the Coming Bear market by Dave Skarica; 228 pages, softcover; ISBN 1-896210-93-7; $29.95 + $5.00 postage/handling + GST.

THE NET EFFECT

Will the Internet be
a Panacea or Curse
for Business and Society
in the Next Ten Years?

By: Iain Williamson

Are you ready for the greatest change to business & society since the Industrial Revolution? Examines some provocative scenarios for the world ten years from now when entire sectors of the economy may be eliminated and other industries will be born. Find out who will be the winners and losers and how it will affect you. Prepare for the dramatic changes that are coming!

THE NET EFFECT - Will the Internet be a Panacea or Curse for Business and Society in the Next 10 Years: by Iain Williamson; 244 pages, softcover, ISBN 1-896210-38-4; $29.95 + $5.00 postage & handling + GST. Order Your Copy Now!

TAX HAVENS
FOR CANADIANS

Ingenious Ways to
Preserve Your Wealth
(and Have Fun Doing It!)

By: Adam Starchild

Are you overtaxed? The offshore solution is your answer. Details on 37 tax havens & what they offer. Tax havens are now within reach of Canada's "middle class". Learn how to save as much as half of your annual tax bill. Protect your assets from professional malpractice suits, divorce proceedings, or no-fault liability suits.

Adam Starchild is the author of many dozen books and articles.

TAX HAVENS FOR CANADIANS - Ingenious Ways to Preserve Your Wealth (and Have Fun Doing It!): by Adam Starchild: 341 pages, softcover; ISBN 1-896210-18-X; $48.95 + $5.00 postage/handling + GST. Order Your Copy Now!

ORDER FORM

✓ **YES, <u>rush</u> me the following publications.
My cheque/money order is enclosed.**

- ☐ Start Your Own Business -
  Be Your Own Boss $29.95 $_____
- ☐ Becoming Successful! $39.95   _____
- ☐ Marketing for Beginners $29.95   _____
- ☐ Marketing Beyond 2000 $27.95   _____
- ☐ Successful Direct Mail Marketing in Canada: $19.95   _____
- ☐ Software for Small Business $29.95   _____
- ☐ Are You Ready for Information Warfare? $34.95   _____
- ☐ The Online World: $39.95   _____
- ☐ Cooperative Time Management $34.95   _____
- ☐ The Lean Office $24.95   _____
- ☐ Lean Production $24.95   _____
- ☐ Stock Market Panic! $29.95   _____
- ☐ The Net Effect: $29.95   _____
- ☐ Tax Havens for Canadians: $48.95   _____
- ☐ She Delivers Steel $24.95   _____
- ☐ Speak with Confidence Now! $24.95   _____
- ☐ Let's be Reasonable $29.95   _____
- ☐ Tips for Entrepreneurs $26.95   _____
- ☐ Steps to Starting and Running a
  Successful Business in Canada: $34.95   _____
- ☐ Checklist for Going into Business: $19.95   _____
- ☐ Make it on Your Own! $29.95   _____
- ☐ Your Guide to Starting & Self-Financing
  Your Own Business in Canada: $24.95   _____
- ☐ Your Guide to Preparing a Plan to Raise
  Money for Your Own Business: $24.95   _____
- ☐ Your Guide to Raising Venture Capital
  for Your Own Business in Canada: $29.95   _____
- ☐ Your Guide to Arranging Bank & Debt
  Financing for Your Own Business: $26.95   _____
- ☐ Your Guide to Financing Business Growth
  by Selling a Piece of the Pie: $18.95   _____
- ☐ Your Guide to Government Financial
  Assistance for Business in..._____:
  (please fill in Province/Territory) $39.95   _____
- ☐ Your Guide to Canadian Export Financing: $26.95   _____
- ☐ Market Overseas with Canadian
  Government Help: $19.95   _____
- ☐ Reach the Global Marketplace: $24.95   _____
- ☐ The Basics for Sales Success $24.95   _____
- ☐ Selling by Mail Order & Independence: $16.95   _____
- ☐ Evaluating Franchise Opportunities: $19.95   _____
- ☐ Your Homebased Business Plan -Also-
  Working With Your Banker: $14.95   _____
- ☐ Shoplifting, Security, Curtailing Crime
  Inside and Out: $29.95
- ☐ Meeting the Samurai: $19.95

CONTINUED ON NEXT PAGE

Order Form Cont:

- ☐ Are You Ready for Information Warfare? $34.95 _____
- ☐ Canadian Business Owners Guide to Patents for Inventions & New Products: $48.00 _____
- ☐ Can You Make Money with Your Idea or Invention? $24.95 _____
- ☐ How to Sell Yourself Into A Job: $29.95 _____
- ☐ Success is the Best Revenge: $39.95 _____
- ☐ How to Get a Job: English only $14.95 _____
- ☐ How to Get a Job: French\English $24.95 _____
- ☐ The Internet Job Search Guide $29.95 _____
- ☐ How to Get a Really Great Job! $29.95 _____
- ☐ 30 Minutes to a Better Job! $9.95 _____
- ☐ The Canadian Business Owners Guide to Salary Administration: $39.95 _____
- ☐ The Ontario Business Owners Guide on How to Meet the Challenge of Pay Equity: $49.95 _____

ADD Postage & Handling at $5.00 on first title: **$5.00**

and ADD $2.00 postage/handling per title thereafter _____

SUB-TOTAL _____

ADD 7% GST _____

PAYMENT ENCLOSED _____

Name_____

Organization_____

Street_____

City/Town_____

Prov_____ Postal Code_____

Phone_____

Mail To:

PRODUCTIVE PUBLICATIONS

P.O. Box 7200, Station A, Toronto, Ontario M5W 1X8
Phone: (416) 483-0634 Fax: (416) 322-7434

Our 14th Year Helping Canadians with the New Economy

Order Now - Thank You!

MONEY BACK GUARANTEE

I understand that if I am not completely satisfied, I may return any book within 100 days of receipt for a full refund with no questions asked.

The Canadian Business Owners Guide to Salary Administration

This book shows you how to implement a practical salary administration scheme for your employees. It is written in an easy to follow, step-by-step format that you can easily adapt.

It contains numerous examples, together with practical exercises to assist you in understanding the concepts involved.

The Canadian Business Owners Guide to Salary Administration prepared by Entrepreneurial Business Consultants of Canada; 164 pages; ISBN 0-920847-11-0; softcover: $39.95 + $5.00 postage/handling + GST. Order now!

The Ontario Business Owners Guide on How to Meet the Challenge of Pay Equity

Provides you with a step-by-step guide on how to implement a salary administration scheme that will satisfy the requirements of the Ontario Act. It shows you how to prepare a pay equity plan.

The Ontario Business Owners Guide on How to Meet the Challenge of Pay Equity prepared by Entrepreneurial Business Consultants of Canada; 260 pgs; ISBN 0920847-12-9; softcover price: $49.95 + $5.00 postage/handling + GST. Order yours now

Do You Know Someone Else Who Would Like a Free Catalogue?

You may have a relative, friend or colleague who is looking for a job or wants to start a business. Do they hold mutual funds or stocks and are worried about preserving their hard-earned money? Do they feel that they are paying too much in taxes and would like to know about tax havens?

Maybe they want to speak better in public or they have to deal with difficult people. Maybe they supervise work in an office or a factory and want to learn about co-operative time management or Japanese just-in-time techniques.

You can have a catalogue sent to them at no cost by calling toll-free leaving their name and address on our automated catalogue request lines:

In Canada call: 1-800-829-1317 (24 hours)
In the USA call: 1-800-850-4636 (24 hours)

PLEASE NOTE: these lines are for catalogue requests only!